I Peter: faith tested, future triumphant

A COMMENTARY BY
WILLIAM MACDONALD

Harold Shaw
Publishers
Wheaton, Illinois

Unless otherwise indicated, the text is taken from The New American Standard Bible, by permission of the Lockman Foundation

Copyright © 1972 by William MacDonald

Library of Congress Catalog Card Number: 72-94099 ISBN 0-87788-675-X

Printed in the United States of America

CONTENTS

Introduction/   5

Chapter 1   I Peter 1:1-25/   **9**

Chapter 2   I Peter 2:1-25/   **33**

Chapter 3   I Peter 3:1-22/   **61**

Chapter 4   I Peter 4:1-19/   **89**

Chapter 5   I Peter 5:1-14/   **101**

Bibliography/   111

Introduction

This epistle claims to have been written by Peter. If the claim is true, we expect to find references to Peter's life and ministry in the letter. And we are not disappointed. There are definite internal indications that Peter was indeed the author.

In 1:8 the writer implies that he had seen Jesus in a way his readers had not. He says, "... *you* have not seen Him," not "... *we* have not seen Him." We shall see in other passages that the writer had companied with the Lord.

The first ten verses of chapter 2 present Christ as the Cornerstone, and thus take us back to the incident at Caesarea Philippi (Matt. 16:13-20). When Peter confessed Jesus as the Christ, the Son of the living God, the Lord Jesus announced that His church would be built on that foundation, that is, on the truth that Christ is the Son of the living God. He is the Cornerstone and Foundation of the church.

The reference to living stones in 2:5 recalls the incident in John 1:42 where Simon's name was changed to Cephas, which means *stone*. Through faith in Christ, Peter became a living stone. It is not surprising that he has so much to say about stones in chapter 2.

In 2:7, the writer quotes Psalm 118:22:
The stone which the builders rejected, this became the very cornerstone.

This is the same passage which Peter quoted when he was arraigned before the rulers, elders and scribes in Jerusalem (Acts 4:11).

As we hear Peter advising his readers to submit to governmental authorities (2:13-17), we think back to that time when he did not submit, but cut off the ear of the high priest's slave (John 18:10). So his advice, in addition to being inspired, has the ring of practical experience behind it.

Chapter 2:21-24 seems to indicate direct knowledge of the trial of the Lord Jesus. Peter could never forget the meek endurance and the silent suffering of the Savior.

In 2:24 we have a reference to the mode of Jesus' death —by crucifixion. The description seems to echo Peter's words in Acts 5:30 and 10:39.

When Peter spoke of his readers returning to the Shepherd and Guardian of their souls (2:25), he might well have been thinking of his own restoration (John 21:15-19), following his denial of the Lord.

The reminder that "love covers a multitude of sins" (4:8) might refer back to Peter's questions, "Lord, how often shall my brother sin against me and I forgive him? Up to seven times?" Jesus said to him, "I do not say to you, up to seven times, but up to seventy times seven" (Matt. 18:21-22). In other words, indefinitely.

In 4:16 we are told that if anyone suffers as a Christian, he should not be ashamed, but in that name he should glorify God. Compare this with Acts 5:40-42 where Peter and the other apostles, after having been flogged, left the Council, "rejoicing that they had been considered worthy to suffer shame for His name."

The writer of the epistle identifies himself as a witness of the sufferings of Christ (5:1). The following expression "a partaker also of the glory that is to be revealed" may be an allusion to the transfiguration. Peter was present, of course, on both occasions.

The gentle, pastoral counsel "... shepherd the flock of God among you" (5:2) reminds us of the Savior's words to Peter, "Tend My lambs.... Shepherd My sheep.... Tend My sheep" (John 21:15-17).

The language of 5:5, "... clothe yourselves with humility toward one another" is strongly reminiscent of the incident in John 13 where Jesus clothed Himself with the apron of a slave and washed the disciples' feet.

In fact, the whole section on pride and humility (5:5-6) is all the more meaningful when we remember Peter's proud assertion that he would never deny the Lord (Mark 14:29-31) and his subsequent threefold denial of the Savior (Mark 14:67-72).

A final reference that may relate to Peter's experience is found in 5:8: "Your adversary, the devil, prowls about like a roaring lion, seeking someone to devour." When Peter wrote this, was he thinking of the time when Jesus said to him, "Simon, Simon, behold, Satan has demanded permission to sift you like wheat ... " (Luke 22:31)?

1

I/Introduction (1:1-2)
A/ The Writer (v. 1a): *Peter, an apostle of Jesus Christ,*
B/ The Recipients (vv. 1b-2c): *to those who reside as aliens,*
1/Earthly Location (v. 1c): *scattered throughout Pontus, Galatia, Cappadocia, Asia, and Bithynia,*
2/Divine Calling (vv. 1d-2c):
a/Chosen (vv. 1d-2a): *who are chosen according to the foreknowledge of God the Father,*
b/Sanctified (v. 2b): *by the sanctifying work of the Spirit,*
c/Converted (v. 2c): *that you may obey Jesus Christ and be sprinkled with His blood:*
C/ The Greeting (v. 2d): *May grace and peace be yours in fullest measure.*

1:1 The beloved fisherman introduces himself as an apostle of Jesus Christ. He had been commissioned by the Lord Jesus as one of the original Twelve, called to be the herald of a glorious, transforming message. By responding to the divine tap on the shoulder, he had become a fisher of men.

All believers are called to represent Christ's interests here on earth. We are all supposed to be missionaries, whether at home or abroad. This is the central purpose of our life as Jesus' followers; all else is subordinate.

The letter is addressed to the aliens or foreigners scattered throughout Pontus, Galatia, Cappadocia, Asia and Bithynia. Who were these exiles? They were Jewish believers who had been dispersed throughout Asia Minor by persecution. But how do we know they were *Jewish* Christians? One key is found in James 1:1, where the word "dispersed" is directly related to the twelve tribes of Israel. Also in John 7:35, the word "dispersion" is used to describe Jews who were scattered among the Greeks. We can be quite sure from these references that Peter's readers were of Jewish birth. And it is clear from the content of the letter that these Jews had become believers in the Lord Jesus Christ. "Scattered in the countries, and yet gathered in God's election, chosen or picked out; strangers to men among whom they dwelt, but *known* and *foreknown* to God; removed from their own country, to which men have naturally an unalterable affection, but made heirs of a better" (F.B. Meyer).

It was fitting that Peter should write to Jewish believers. He had been chosen by the Lord to be an apostle to the circumcision, that is, to the people of Israel (Gal. 2:7-8). It was he who first broke the good news to them on the day of Pentecost (Acts 2).

Pontus, Galatia, Cappadocia, Asia and Bithynia were Roman provinces in the northern part of Asia Minor, or what is now Turkey (see any Bible Map of Mediterranean Lands illustrating the Acts and the Epistles).

1:1*d*-2 The recipients of the letter are further designated as:

    chosen according to the foreknowledge of God the Father
    sanctified by the Spirit
    obedient to Jesus Christ
    sprinkled with His blood

In this fourfold progression we have a vignette of their salvation which involved all three Persons of the Trinity.

First of all, they were chosen by God the Father. This simply means that in a past eternity, God elected them to belong to Himself. The doctrine of divine election is not always popular, but it does have this virtue—it allows God to be God. Attempts to make it palatable to man only succeed in detracting from the sovereignty of God.

While the Bible teaches divine election, it never teaches divine reprobation, that is, that God chooses some to be damned. God makes a bona fide offer of salvation to all. Anyone can be saved by believing on the Lord Jesus Christ. If men are lost, it is their own fault, not God's.

Any difficulty in reconciling God's election and man's free will lies in man's mind, not in God's. The Bible teaches both doctrines, and we should believe both. The truth lies in both extremes, not somewhere between them.

God's choice is said to be according to His foreknowledge. Some understand this to mean that God elected those whom He foreknew would trust the Savior. Others say that God knew very well that, left to himself, no sinner would trust the Savior, and so in His foreknowledge He marked out certain ones to be trophies of His grace. While there is unutterable mystery in God's choice, we can be sure that there is nothing unfair about it.

The second step in salvation is sanctification by the Spirit. This particular aspect of sanctification takes place before conversion.[1] It is a ministry of the Holy Spirit by which He sets people apart to belong to God (see also 2 Thess.

---

[1] *There are other forms of sanctification which take place later. When a person is born again, he becomes* positionally *sanctified because he is "in Christ" (Heb. 10:10, 14). Throughout his Christian life he should experience* practical *sanctification, that is, the process of becoming more like Christ (1 Pet. 1:15). In heaven he will achieve* perfect *sanctification, for he will never again sin (Col. 1:22).*

2:13). It logically follows election by God the Father. In *eternity* God foreknew and chose men. In *time* the Holy Spirit operates to make that election real in the lives of the individuals concerned.

The third step in the soul's salvation is the sinner's response to the work of the Holy Spirit. It is described in 1:2 as obedience to Jesus Christ. This means obeying the gospel by repenting of one's sins and receiving Jesus Christ as Lord and Savior. The concept of the gospel as something to be obeyed is a common one in the New Testament (see Rom. 2:8; 2 Thess. 1:8).

Finally, there is the sprinkling with His blood. We must not take this with absolute literalness and insist that when a person is saved, he is actually sprinkled with the blood of Jesus. This is figurative language. What it does say is that as soon as a person obeys the gospel, he receives all the benefits which flow from the shedding of Christ's blood on Calvary. The Savior's blood was shed once for all over 1900 years ago; it will never be shed again. But we receive forgiveness, redemption, and the other innumerable blessings that flow from that crimson tide as soon as we believe on Him.

Having traced the four steps in his readers' spiritual birth, Peter now wishes that grace and peace might be theirs in fullest measure. They have already experienced the grace of God in salvation and the resulting peace with God. But day by day they will need grace or strength for the Christian life, and peace in the midst of a turbulent society. That is what the apostle wishes for them here in fullest abundance. James Denny said that "grace is the first and last word of the Gospel; and peace—perfect spiritual soundness—is the finished work of grace."

II/The Privileged Position Of The Believer (1:3-12)
A/ The Divine Source (v. 3a): *Blessed be the God and Father of our Lord Jesus Christ,*
B/ The Divine Virtue Displayed (v. 3b): *who according to His great mercy*
C/ The Spiritual Change Produced (v. 3c): *has caused us to be born again*
D/ The Present Benefit (v. 3d):
   1/Its Nature: *to a living hope*
   2/Its Guarantee: *through the resurrection of Jesus Christ from the dead,*
E/ The Future Inheritance (vv. 4-5): *to obtain* an inheritance
   1/Its Unique Character (v. 4a): which is
   a/Death-Proof: *imperishable*
   b/Sin-Proof: *and undefiled*
   c/Age-Proof: *and will not fade away,*
   2/Its Reserved Place (v. 4b): *reserved in heaven*
   3/Its Preserved People (vv. 4c-5): *for you,*
   a/The Keeping Power (v. 5a): *who are protected by the power of God*
   b/The Human Response (v. 5b): *through faith*
   c/The Ultimate End (v. 5c): *for a salvation*
   d/The Impending Revelation (v. 5d): *ready to be revealed in the last time.*
F/ The Present Joy (v. 6a): *In this you greatly rejoice,*
G/ The Accompanying Testings (vv. 6b-7):
   1/Their Temporary Character (v. 6b): *even though now for a little while, if necessary,*
   2/Their Diverse Forms (v. 6c): *you have been distressed by various trials,*
   3/Their Final Outcome (v. 7):
   a/The Proving Of Faith: *that the proof of your faith,*
   b/The Preciousness Of Faith: being *more precious than gold which is perishable, even though tested by fire,*

c/The Praise Of Faith: *may be found to result in praise and glory and honor at the revelation of Jesus Christ;*
H/　The Glorious Savior (v. 8):
　　　1/Unseen: *and though you have not seen Him,*
　　　2/Yet Loved: *you love Him,*
　　　3/Unseen: *and though you do not see Him now,*
　　　4/Yet Trusted: *but believe in Him,*
　　　5/And Enjoyed: *you greatly rejoice with joy inexpressible and full of glory.*
I/　The Believer's Reward (v. 9): *obtaining as the outcome of your faith the salvation of your souls.*
J/　The Prophets' Problem (vv. 10-11): *As to this salvation, the prophets who prophesied of the grace that* would come *to you made careful search and inquiry,*
　　　1/The Unknown Identity Of The Messiah (v. 11a): *seeking to know what person*
　　　2/The Unknown Time Of The Messiah (v. 11b): *or time*
　　　3/The Inspiring Spirit Of The Messiah (v. 11c): *the Spirit of Christ within them was indicating as He predicted*
　　　4/The Predicted Sufferings Of The Messiah (v. 11d): *the sufferings of Christ*
　　　5/The Predicted Glory Of The Messiah (v. 11e): *and the glories to follow.*
K/　The Problem Resolved (v. 12):
　　　1/The People Served: *It was revealed to them that they were not serving themselves but you*
　　　2/The Prophecy Fulfilled:
　　　a/The Apostolic Message: *in these things which now have been announced to you*
　　　b/The Apostolic Messengers: *through those who preached the gospel to you*
　　　c/The Apostolic Power: *by the Holy Spirit sent from heaven,—*
　　　d/The Angelic Curiosity: *things into which angels long to look.*

1:3 Beginning with verse 3 and continuing through verse 12, Peter sets forth the unique glories of our salvation. He begins by calling for praise to be given to the Author of salvation—the God and Father of our Lord Jesus Christ. This title presents God in a twofold relationship to the Lord Jesus. The name "God of our Lord Jesus Christ" emphasizes the humanity of the Savior. The name "Father" underlines the deity of God's Son. The full name of the Son is given:

>Lord/the One with exclusive right to rule in hearts and lives.

>Jesus/the One who saves His people from their sins.

>Christ/God's anointed One who has been exalted to heaven's highest place.

It is by God's great mercy that we have been born anew to a living hope through the resurrection of Jesus Christ from the dead. God is the source of this salvation. His great mercy is its cause or reason. The new birth is the nature of it. A living hope is its present reward. The resurrection of Christ is the righteous basis of our salvation, as well as the foundation of our living hope.

As sinners, we had no hope beyond the grave. There was nothing ahead for us but the certainty of judgment and fiery indignation. As members of the first creation we were under the sentence of death. But in the redemptive work of Christ, God found a righteous basis upon which He can save ungodly sinners and still be just. Christ has paid the penalty of our sins. Full satisfaction has been made. The claims of justice have been met, and now mercy can flow out to those who obey the gospel. In the resurrection of Christ, God indicated His complete satisfaction with the sacrificial work of His Son. "The resurrection is God's 'Amen' to Christ's cry, 'It is finished.' " Also, that resurrection is a pledge that all who die in Christ will be raised from among the dead. This is our living hope—the expectation of being taken home to heaven to be with Christ and to be like Him forever. F. B. Meyer calls the living hope "the link between our present and future."

1:4 The next two verses describe this future aspect of our salvation. When we are born again we have the certain hope of an inheritance in heaven. The inheritance includes all that the believer will enjoy in heaven for eternity, all that will be his through Christ (Ps. 16:5). The inheritance is imperishable, undefiled and unfading:

    1/Imperishable means that it is incorruptible. It can never corrode, or crack, or decay. It is death-proof.

    2/Undefiled means that the inheritance itself is in perfect condition. No tarnish nor stain can dim its purity. It is sin-proof.

    3/Unfading means that it can never suffer variations in value, glory or beauty. It is time-proof.

Earthly inheritances are uncertain at the best. Sometimes the value of an estate drops sharply because of market declines. Sometimes wills are successfully contested by parties not mentioned in them. Sometimes people are deprived of an inheritance because of legal technicalities. But this divine inheritance is not subject to any of the changes of time, and there are no loopholes in the believer's title to it. It is kept in the safety-vault of heaven for the child of God.

1:5 Not only is the inheritance guarded for Christians, but they are guarded or kept for it. In this life an heir may die before an inheritance is divided. But the same grace that preserves the heavenly inheritance preserves us as heirs to enjoy it.

God's election of His people can never be frustrated. Those who were chosen in eternity past are saved in time now and kept for eternity to come. The believer in Christ is eternally secure.

But notice that there is a human as well as a divine side to eternal security. We are kept by the power of God—that is the divine side, but it is through faith—that is the human side. This does not mean that a person is saved only as long as he exersives faith. The Bible teaches that where there is true faith, there will be continuance. Saving faith always has the quality of permanence.

The child of God is guarded by God's power unto a salvation ready to be revealed in the last time. This, of course, refers to salvation in its fullest sense, to salvation in its three tenses:

1/A Christian *was saved* from the penalty of sin the moment he first trusted the Savior (Ephesians 2:8).

2/He *is saved* daily from the power of sin as he allows the Savior to live His life through him (Romans 5:10).

3/He *will be saved* from the presence of sin at the time of the rapture (Hebrews 9:28). His body will be changed and glorified, and be forever free from sin, sickness and death. This future tense of salvation also includes the time when the saints will return to earth with Christ and will be clearly shown to be sons of God (1 John 3:2).

1:6 Because of this hope of the redemption of the body and of a glorious inheritance, believers can be joyful even in the midst of sorrow. The Jewish Christians to whom Peter was writing were suffering intense persecution because of their testimony for Christ. Peter reminds them of one of the delightful paradoxes of Christianity—joy in the midst of sorrow. On the one hand they can rejoice in the prospect of a kept inheritance for a kept people. On the other hand, they can find joy in the knowledge that the various trials are only for a little while whereas the glory will be forever (see 2 Corinthians 4:17). Commenting on the presence of joy in the midst of grief caused by numerous trials, J. H. Jowett wrote: "I never expected to find a fountain in so unpromising a waste."

1:7 There is further comfort for suffering saints in the knowledge that their sufferings are neither purposeless nor fruitless. The sufferings of the ungodly are only a foretaste of the pangs of hell which they will endure eternally. This is not true for the Christian. One of the many beneficial purposes of afflictions in this life for the child of God is to test the genuineness of his faith. Peter contrasts our faith with gold. Of all the substances known to man, gold is one of the most imperishable. It can be subjected to intense heat and might seem to be indestructible. But the truth is that gold wastes away through use, through pressure, through fire.

True faith is indestructible. The believer may undergo severe tests and trials, but instead of destroying his faith, they become food for faith to feed on. Job probably sustained heavier losses in one day than any other man in the history of the world, yet he was able to say, "Though He slay me, I will hope in Him" (Job 13:15). The three men in the Babylonian furnace were literally tried by fire. The fire proved their faith to be real. Also it burned away the ropes that held them, setting them free (Daniel 3:12-30). And during their flaming ordeal, they had the companionship of One "like unto the Son of God." The genuineness of faith can be proved only by fire. When prevailing conditions are favorable, it might be popular and easy to be a Christian. But when public confession of Christ brings persecution and suffering, then the casual followers drift away and are lost in the crowd. "A religion which costs nothing is worth nothing." Faith which refuses to pay the price is spurious. It is the kind of say-so faith that James condemns.

Genuine faith will result in praise and glory and honor when Jesus Christ is revealed. This simply means that God will reward every instance of faith that stood the test. He will praise those who are joyful though surrounded by trouble.

He will award glory and honor to tried and suffering believers who were able to accept their tribulations as a vote of confidence from Him.

This will be apparent when Jesus Christ comes back to the earth to reign as King of kings and Lord of lords, and all those whom the world rejected will be shown clearly to be sons of God. A comparison of Scripture indicates that rewards will be announced at the judgment seat of Christ, in heaven, after the rapture. But the public display of these rewards apparently takes place at the second advent of Christ.

1:8 Peter now discusses the present enjoyment of our **salvation**—Christ taken by faith. Though we have never seen **Him** with our physical eyes, we love Him. He has made Himself to us:

> . . . a living bright reality,
> More present to faith's vision keen
> Than any earthly object seen,
> More dear, more intimately nigh,
> Than e'en the closest earthly tie.

Though we do not see Him now, yet we believe in Him. That is how we enter into the blessedness which He mentioned to Thomas, "Blessed are they who did not see, and yet believed" (John 20:29).

"People talk a lot about love, but the true test of love to God and Christ is, that in the trial it says—'I would not lose the favor and smile of God, so will rather suffer than grieve Him.' Love will be content with a crust and the smile of God, rather than a better position and the popularity of the world without it. Such tests must come to all the true children of God; they winnow the chaff from the wheat. The gold comes out from the fire tried, and purified from its dross" (Wm. Lincoln).

Believing on **Him we rejoice with** "joy inexpressible and

full of glory." To be united to Him through faith is to have uninterrupted and eternal contact with the fountain of all pure joy. The Christian's joy is not dependent on earthly circumstances. It is dependent on the risen, exalted Christ at God's right hand. It is no more possible to rob a saint of his joy than it is to unseat Christ from His place of glory. The two stand together.

1:9 Next, Peter deals with the present outcome of faith—the salvation of the soul. The salvation of the body is still future; it will take place when Christ comes for His saints. But as soon as we trust Christ by faith, we receive the salvation of our souls. The word here refers to the non-material part of man, his person, his being apart from his body. It is the soul which is separated from the body at the time of death. In this passage it includes the spirit, by which we have God-consciousness. The soul is saved at the time of the new birth.

1:10 This salvation was the subject of many Old Testament prophecies. God's ancient spokesmen foretold the undeserved favor which we would receive. But they did not fully understand what they were writing (see Daniel 12:8).

1:11 They apparently did not understand two things:
    1. The identity of the Person who would appear as Messiah.
    2. The time of His appearance. They were inspired by the Spirit of God to foretell the sufferings of the Messiah and the glories that would follow. But they did not understand that these two events would be separated by at least 1900 years. As has often been pictured, they saw the two mountain peaks—
    a. Calvary, where Jesus suffered,
    b. Olivet, where He will return in glory.

But they did not see the valley which lay between. That is, the present age of grace, in which we find ourselves able to see both events, one past, one still future, with a clearer perspective than they.

1:12 The Spirit of God mysteriously communicated to them the knowledge that they were serving generations yet unborn. While the prophets' words had meaning for their own generation, they were aware that the full meaning of the prophecies was not exhausted by events in their day.

This, of course, raises questions. Were not the Old Testament prophets familiar with the truth of justification by faith? What was it that they did not understand about our salvation? In what sense did they serve us rather than themselves?

William Lincoln says, "The fulness of God's grace could not appear till Christ came. God could and did save sinners and take them to heaven, as He did Enoch before, but union with Christ and all that such union implies, could not be until Christ died and rose again. O how God delights to heap honour upon His Son!"

The things that were veiled to the prophets were now revealed. The Holy Spirit came down from heaven on the day of Pentecost. He empowered the apostles to preach the good news that Jesus of Nazareth was the predicted Messiah, that He had died for the sins of men, had been buried and had been raised the third day. They announced that salvation was offered as a free gift through faith in Christ. They declared that God's purpose during this age is to gather out of the nations a people for His name, and that the Lord Jesus would return to earth one day to take the scepter of universal government.

The immense privilege of believers in this age is seen not only in the fact that they understand clearly what was veiled from the **prophets, but also** in the fact that angels long to look into these truths of salvation. Angels have a prominent place in the New Testament as well as in the Old. They are mentioned in connection with the birth of Christ, His temptation, His agony in Gethsemane and His resurrection. But as far as we know, there is no redemption for angels that have fallen. Christ did not come to intervene on behalf of angels, but on behalf of Abraham's descendants (Hebrews 2:16). The church is an object lesson to angels, setting forth the manifold wisdom of God (Ephesians 3:10). But it is not for them to know "the joy that our salvation brings."

III/The Believer's Conduct In The Light Of His Position (1:13—2:3)

A/ The Girded Mind (1:13a): *Therefore, gird your minds for action,*

B/ The Sober Mind (1:13b): *keep sober* in spirit,

C/ The Optimistic Mind (1:13c): *fix your hope completely on the grace to be brought to you at the revelation of Jesus Christ.*

D/ The Obedient Mind (1:14-16): *As obedient children,*

1/Non-Conformity To Evil (v. 14b): *do not be conformed to the former lusts* which were yours *in your ignorance,*

2/Conformity To Holiness (vv. 15-16):

a/The Example (v. 15a): *but like the Holy One who called you,*

b/The Exhortation (v. 15b): *be holy yourselves also*

c/The Extent (v. 15c): *in all* your *behavior;*

d/The Explanation (v. 16): *because it is written,* "You shall be holy, for I am holy."

E/ The Reverent Mind (1:17-21):

1/The Father's Impartial Judgment (v. 17a): *And if you address as Father the One who impartially judges according to each man's work,*

2/The Child's Appropriate Behavior (v. 17b): *conduct*

yourselves in fear during the time of your stay upon earth;
3/The Savior's Glorious Redemption (vv. 18-21):
a/The Fact of our Ransom (v. 18*a*, RSV): *You know that you were ransomed*
b/The Bondage From Which Delivered (v. 18*b*, RSV): *from the futile ways inherited from your fathers,*
c/The Ransom Price (vv. 18*c*-19, RSV):
    [1] Not Perishable Metal (v. 18*c*, RSV): *not with perishable things such as silver or gold,*
    [2] But Precious Blood (v. 19, RSV): *but with the precious blood of Christ, like that of a lamb without blemish or spot.*
d/The Illustrious Redeemer (v. 20):
    [1] His Foreordination: *For He was foreknown before the foundation of the world,*
    [2] His Manifestation: *but has appeared in these last times for the sake of you*
e/The Unshakeable Confidence (v. 21):
    [1] Its Mediator: *who through Him*
    [2] Its Object: *are believers in God,*
    [3] Its Basis: *who raised Him from the dead and gave Him glory,*
    [4] Its Result: *so that your faith and hope are in God.*

F/   The Loving Mind (1:22—2:3):
1/The Nature of the New Birth (1:22*a*, RSV):
a/The Cleansing Effected: *Having purified your souls*
b/The Means Employed: *by your obedience to the truth*
c/The Goal Envisaged: *for a sincere love of the brethren,*
2/The Resulting Obligation to Love (1:22*b*, RSV): *love one another*
a/Warmly: *earnestly*
b/Deeply: *from the heart.*
3/The Seed of the New Birth (1:23-25): *for you have*

been born again
a/Imperishable (v. 23b): *not of seed which is perishable but imperishable,*
b/Living (v. 23c): that is, *through the living*
c/Abiding (vv. 23d-25a): *and abiding word of God.*
  [1] Transient Man (v. 24a): *For, "All flesh is like grass, And all its glory like the flower of grass.*
  [2] Short-lived Vegetation (v. 24b): *The grass withers, And the flower falls off,*
  [3] Eternal Word (v. 25a): *But the word of the Lord abides forever."*
d/Good News (v. 25b): *And this is the word which was preached to you.*

1:13 Beginning with this verse, there is a change in the emphasis of the epistle. Peter has been dealing with the glories of our salvation. At this point, he launches into a series of exhortations based upon the foregoing. "The present appeal is based upon the introductory evangel. Spiritual impulse is created by the momentum of superlative facts. The dynamic of duty is born in the heart of the gospel" (Jowett).

First, Peter urges the saints to have a "girded" mind. The girding of the mind is an interesting figure of speech. In eastern lands, men wore long, flowing robes. When they wanted to walk in haste or with a minimum of hindrance, they would tie the robe up around their waist with a belt (see Exodus 12:11). In this way they girded up their loins.

But what does Peter mean, "gird your minds for action"? As they went out into a hostile world, believers were to avoid panic and distraction. In times of persecution, there is always the tendency to become rattled and confused. A girded mind is one that is strong, composed, cool and ready for action. It is unimpeded by the distraction of human fear or persecution.

This state of **mental solidarity** is further encouraged by the words "keep sober in spirit." This means self-control in contrast to hysteria. The sober spirit is poised and stable.

Next the saints are urged to have the optimistic, on-looking mind: "fix your hope completely on the grace to be brought to you at the revelation of Jesus Christ." The assurance of Christ's return is here held out as a compelling motive for endurance through the storms and tribulations of life. The revelation of Jesus Christ is generally taken to refer to His coming back to earth when He will be revealed in glory. However, it could also refer to the rapture when Christ will come for His saints.

1:14 In verses 14-16, the subject is the obedient mind. Those who are children of obedience should not indulge in the sins which characterized them in their former life. Now that they are Christians, they should pattern their life after the one whose name they bear. If they conform to the ungodly world, they are denying their heavenly character.

The things they did in the days of their ignorance should be put away now that they have been illuminated by the Holy Spirit. The former lusts of their ignorance means the sins they indulged in while they were still ignorant of God.

1:15 Instead of imitating the ungodly world, its fads and fashions, its modes and manners, our lives should reproduce the holy character of the One who called us. To be godly means to be God-like. God is holy in all His ways. If we are to be like Him, we must be holy in all that we do and say. In this life we will never be *as* holy as He is, but we should be holy *because* He is.

1:16 At this point, Peter reaches back into the Old Testament for proof that God expects His people to be like Himself. In Leviticus 11:44, Jehovah said, "Be holy; for I am holy."

Christians are empowered to live holy lives by the indwelling Holy Spirit. Old Testament saints did not have this help and blessing. But since we are more privileged, we are also more responsible. The verse Peter quotes from Leviticus acquires a new depth of meaning in the New Testament. As someone has said, it is the difference between the formal and the vital. Holiness was God's ideal in the Old Testament. It has assumed a concrete, everyday quality with the coming of the spirit of truth.

1:17 Not only are we exhorted to holiness but also to a reverent mind. This means a respectful fear, a deep appreciation of who God is. It especially means a realization that the One whom we address as Father is the same One who judges His children impartially according to their deeds. As we realize the extent of His knowledge and the accuracy of His judgment, we should live with a wholesome fear of displeasing Him. The Father judges His own in this life; He has committed the judgment of sinners to the Lord Jesus (John 5:22).

"He is looking on, taking notice of all, whether there is integrity of purpose, intelligence of mind, and desire of heart to please Him" (William Lincoln).

We are to pass the time of our stay upon earth in fear. Christians are not at home in this world. We are living in a foreign country, exiled from heaven. We should not settle down as if this were our permanent dwelling. Neither should we imitate the behavior of the earth-dwellers. Ever and always we should remember our heavenly destiny and behave ourselves as citizens of heaven.

1:18 Before their conversion, believers were no different from the rest of the people in the world. Their talk and their walk were as empty and trivial as that of men around them.

Their unconverted days are here described as "your futile way of life inherited from your forefathers."

But they had been ransomed from that futile existence by a tremendous transaction. They had been rescued from the slavery of world-conformity by the payment of an infinite ransom-price. Was it by silver and gold that these kidnap-victims had been freed? (See Exodus 30:15).

1:19 No, it was with the precious blood of Christ—like the blood of a perfect, unblemished lamb. Christ is a lamb without blemish or spot, that is, He is absolutely perfect, inwardly and outwardly. If a believer is ever tempted to return to worldly pleasures and amusements, to adopt worldly modes and patterns, to become like the world in its false ways, he should remember that Christ shed His blood to deliver him from that kind of life. To go back to the world is to re-cross the great gulf that was bridged for us at staggering cost. But even more—it is positive disloyalty to the Savior.

"Reason back from the greatness of the sacrifice to the greatness of the sin. Then determine to be done forever with that which cost God's Son His life."

1:20 Christ's work for us was no afterthought on God's part. The Redeemer was destined to die for us before the world was created. But at the end of the times, that is, at the end of the dispensation of law, He appeared from heaven to rescue us from our former way of life. "In these last times— the world's moral history was closed at the cross of Christ. It has shown itself fully and got to its end before God" (William Lincoln).

Peter adds these considerations to impress us even more deeply with the importance of making a clean break with the world system from which Christ died to deliver us. We are in the world but not of it. We must not isolate ourselves from unregenerate **men, but rather** carry the gospel to them. Yet in our dealings and relationships with them, we must never share in or condone their sins. We are to show by our lives that we are children of God. The moment we become like the world, our testimony is weakened. There is no incentive for worldlings to be converted if they cannot see a difference—a change for the better in our lives.

1:21 Loyalty to the Lord Jesus is further demanded by the fact that it is through Him we have come to believe in God. He is the One who has revealed the Father's heart to us. "It is not by creation nor providence nor law that man knows God, but by Christ" (W.T.P. Wolston).

The Father indicated His complete satisfaction with Christ's redeeming work by raising Him out from among the dead ones and honoring Him with the place of highest glory in heaven.

The result of all this is that our faith and hope are in God. It is in Him, not in the present evil world system, that we live and move and have our being.

1:22 Now the apostle Peter urges his readers to have the loving mind (1:22—2:3). First, he describes the new birth and points out that one of the changes that it brings is love for our brothers (1:22*a*). Next, he presses home the obligation to love (1:22*b*). Again he reverts to the new birth, and especially to the seed from which this new life has grown—the Word of God (1:23-25). And once again he emphasizes the obligations that rest on those who have received the Word (2:1-3).

In 1:22*a*, Peter first describes the new birth: "Since you have . . . purified your souls. . . ." We understand, of course, that it is God who purifies our souls when we are saved; in the strict sense, we do not have the power for personal purity. But in this figure of speech those of us who have experienced purification are said to have attained it.

The means employed in this purification is "obedience to the truth." This is the second time that Peter describes saving faith as an act of obedience (see 1:2). In Romans, Paul twice uses the phrase "the obedience of faith." The lesson is that in our thinking we should not try to separate belief and obedience. True faith is obeying faith.

One of the goals of the new birth is "sincere love of the brethren." In a very real sense, we are saved in order to love all our fellow-Christians. By this love, we know that we have passed out of death into life (1 John 3:14), and by it, the world knows that we are disciples of the Lord Jesus (John 13:35).

So the exhortation follows quite naturally: "Fervently love one another from the heart." This is one of the many instances in the New Testament where a declarative statement becomes the basis for an imperative. The declaration is this: "Since you have ... purified your souls for a sincere love of the brethren...." Then the imperative: "fervently love one another from the heart." The positional forms the basis for the practical.

While it is difficult to differentiate precisely between "fervently" and "from the heart," the words in combination certainly mean that our love should be warm, wholehearted, with all our strength, earnest, and unceasing.

The exhortation to love one another is especially timely for a people undergoing persecution because it is well known that "under conditions of hardship, trivial disagreements take on gigantic proportions."

1:23 Again Peter takes his readers back to their new birth, and this time to the seed of that birth, the Word of God. The exhortations in 2:1-3 will be based on this.

The new birth is not brought about by corruptible seed, that is, it is not produced in the same way as a physical birth. Human life is brought into being by means of seed that must obey physical laws of decay and death. The physical life that is produced has the same quality as the seed from which it sprang; it too is of a temporary character.

The new birth is brought about through the Word of God. As men hear or read the Bible they are convicted of their sins, convinced that Christ is the sole and sufficient Savior, and converted to God. No one is ever saved apart from the instrumentality in some way of the incorruptible Word of God.

"It is interesting to note the three 'incorruptible' things we have in this first chapter—an incorruptible inheritance (v. 4), an incorruptible redemption (vv. 18, 19), and an incorruptible word by which we are born (v. 23). Thus we have a nature which is taintless, fitted for the enjoyment of a taintless inheritance and on the basis of an inheritance which can never lose its value. How the stamp of eternal perfection is upon all, and what a fitting companion to those is that incorruptible ornament of a meek and quiet spirit (3:4)" (Samuel Ridout in the Numerical Bible).

The Word lives and abides forever. Though heaven and earth pass away, it will never pass away. It is settled forever in heaven. And the life it produces is eternal also. Those who are born anew through the Word take on the everlasting character of the Word.

In human birth, the seed which produces a child contains, in germ form, all the characteristics of the child. What the child will eventually be is determined by the seed. For our present purposes, it is enough to see that as the seed is perishable, so is the human life which results from it.

1:24 The transitory character of human nature is emphasized by a quotation of Isaiah 40:6-7. Human life is as impermanent as grass. Physical beauty is as short-lived as the flowers of the field. The grass withers away, and the flowers droop and die.

1:25 In contrast, the Word of the Lord endures forever (Isaiah 40:8). And therefore the new life of the believer is equally incorruptible.

This incorruptible Word is the message of good news which was preached to Peter's readers and which caused them to be born again. It was the source of their eternal life.

2

III/The Believer's Conduct In The Light Of His Position (1:13—2:3) (Cont'd)
F/ The Loving Mind (1:22—2:3) (Cont'd)
    4/The Resulting Obligations (2:1-3)
       a/Acts Of Unlove To Put Away (v. 1): *Therefore, putting aside all malice and all guile and hypocrisy and envy and all slander,*
       b/Appetite To Cultivate (vv. 2-3):
          [1] Degree (v. 2a): *like newborn babes,*
          [2] Desire (v. 2b): *long for the pure milk of the word,*
          [3] Object (v. 2c): *that by it you may grow in respect to salvation,*
          [4] Impetus (v. 3): *if you have tasted the kindness of the Lord.*

2:1   Because they are partakers of the divine life described in the closing verses of the first chapter, Christians should put away once for all the following unloving acts:

    Malice—the harboring of evil thoughts against another person. Malice nourishes antagonisms, builds up grudges, and secretly hopes that revenge, harm, or tragedy will overtake another. George Washington Carver was refused admission at a university because he was a Negro. Years later when someone asked him the name of the university, he replied, "Never mind. That doesn't matter now." He harbored no malice.

Guile—any form of deceit, dishonesty and trickery (and what a variety of forms it takes!). Guile falsifies income tax returns, cheats on exams, lies about age, bribes officials, and pulls shady deals in business.

Hypocrisy—insincerity, pretense, sham. The hypocrite is a play-actor, pretending to be someone he is not. He pretends to be happily married when his home is actually a battlefield. He pretends to be spiritual on Sundays but he is as carnal as a goat on weekdays. He pretends interest in others but his motive is always selfish.

Envy—bare-faced jealousy. Vine defines it as the feeling of displeasure produced by observing or hearing of the advantage or prosperity of others. It was envy that caused the chief priests to deliver Jesus up to Pilate for death (Matt. 27:18). Envy is still a killer. Women can look daggers at others because of their better homes and gardens, their smarter clothes, or their superior cooking. A man can praise another fellow's new car or speedboat but what he is thinking is, "I'll show him. I'll get something better."

Slander—backbiting, malicious gossip, recrimination. Slander is the attempt to make oneself look cleaner by slinging mud at someone else. It may take very subtle forms such as, "Yes, she is a lovely person but she has this one failing . . ." and then the knife is deftly thrust into her back. Or it may even have a religious pose: "I mention this only for your prayer fellowship, but did you know that he . . ." and then the character is assassinated.

All these sins are violations of the fundamental commandment to love our neighbor as ourselves. No wonder Peter tells us to decisively rid ourselves of them.

2:2 A second obligation flowing from our new birth is to

have an insatiable craving for the pure spiritual milk of the Word. The sins mentioned in the previous verse stunt spiritual growth; the good Word of God nourishes it.

The phrase "like newborn babes" does not necessarily mean that Peter's readers were new believers; they may have been saved for several years. But young or old in the faith, they thirsted, and should thirst for the Word just as infants cry for milk. We get some idea of the thirst of the healthy baby by the impatient, aggressive, determined way he sucks and swallows.

By the pure spiritual milk a believer grows in or grows up to salvation. Here salvation is used in its ultimate sense— the final and complete deliverance of the believer from the presence of sin at the coming of Christ for His saints (Rom. 13:11; 1 Thess. 4:13-18). This is the goal toward which all spiritual growth in this life is moving.

2:3   "If you have tasted the kindness of the Lord." What a tremendous impetus for thirsting for the pure spiritual milk! The "if" does not express any doubt; we *have* tasted and seen that the Lord is good (Psalm 34:8). His sacrifice for us was an act of unspeakable goodness and kindness (Titus 3:4). What we have already tasted of His kindness should whet our appetites to feed more and more on Him. The sweet taste of nearness to Him should make us dread the thought of ever wandering away from Him.

IV/The Believers' Privileges In The New House And Priesthood (2:4-10)
A/   Christ, The Living Stone (v. 4a): *And coming to Him as to a living stone,*
   1/Rejected Stone (v. 4b): *rejected by men,*
   2/Precious Stone (v. 4c): *but choice and precious in the sight of God,*
B/   The Role Of Believers (v. 5)

        1/Living Stones (v. 5*a*): *you also, as living stones,*
        2/Spiritual House (v. 5*b*): *are being built up as a spiritual house*
        3/Holy Priesthood (v. 5*c-f*): *for a holy priesthood,*
        a/Function (v. 5*d*): *to offer up spiritual sacrifices*
        b/Recipient (v. 5*e*): *acceptable to God*
        c/Mediator (v. 5*f*): *through Jesus Christ.*

C/   Christ, The Cornerstone (v. 6):
        1/Foretold In Scripture: *For* this *is contained in Scripture:*
        2/Divinely Established: *Behold I lay in Zion*
        3/Chosen And Precious: *A Choice stone, A Precious Cornerstone,*
        4/Completely Dependable: *And He who believes in Him shall not be disappointed."*

D/   Christ, The Touchstone (vv. 7-8, RSV):
        1/To Believers (v. 7*a*, RSV): *To you therefore who believe, he is precious,*
        2/To Unbelievers (v. 7*b*-8, RSV): *but for those who do not believe,*
        a/Rejected Stone (v. 7*c*, RSV): *"The very stone which the builders rejected*
        b/Head Stone Of The Corner (v. 7*d*, RSV): *has become the head of the corner,"*
        c/Stumblingstone (v. 8, RSV): *and "A stone that will make men stumble, a rock that will make them fall";*
            [1] Failure: *for they stumble because they disobey the word,*
            [2] Foreordination: *as they were destined to do.*

E/   The Role of Believers (vv. 9-10):
        1/Position (v. 9*a*):
        a/Race: *But you are* A chosen race,
        b/Priesthood: *A Royal Priesthood,*
        c/Nation: *A Holy Nation,*
        d/People: *A People for God's Own Possession,*

2/Function (v. 9*b*): *that you may proclaim the excellencies of Him who has called you out of darkness into His marvelous light:*
3/Transformation (v. 10):
a/Past: *for you once were not a people,*
b/Present: *but now you are the people of God;*
c/Then: *you had not received mercy,*
d/Now: *but now you have received mercy.*

2:4 Now Peter moves from the field of exhortation to a consideration of believers' privileges in the new house (the church) and in the new priesthood.

In the new order Christ is central, and so we come to Him. Because Peter is thinking in terms of a building and of building materials, we are not surprised to find the Lord presented figuratively as the Stone. First He is that living Stone—not an inanimate or dead stone but One who lives in the power of an endless life (Heb. 7:16, KJV).

Incredible as it may seem, He is rejected by men. In their stupid, selfish, amateurish blueprints for life, insignificant, shortsighted men can find no place for their Creator and Redeemer. Just as there was no room for Him in the inn, so there is no place for Him in the plan of their lives!

But it is not man's opinion that counts. In God's sight the Lord Jesus is chosen and precious. He is chosen as not only the suitable Stone but the indispensable One. And His value to God is inestimable; He is precious beyond computation.

If we are going to be used in God's building program we must come to Christ. Our only suitability to be building materials is derived from our identification with Him. We are only important as we contribute to His glory.

2:5 The spiritual house is built up of all who believe in Christ, and is therefore the same as the church. The church has this in common with the temple of the Old Testament that it is the dwelling place of God on earth (1 Kings 6:11-13; Eph. 2:22). But it is contrasted with the temple, a physical, tangible building made of beautiful but lifeless, perishable materials. The church is a structure built of living stones.

Now the figure changes swiftly from the spiritual house to the holy priesthood that functions in connection with the house. Believers are not only living building blocks in the house; they are holy priests as well. Peter did not have to mention the superiority of this new priesthood; it would be obvious to his ex-Jewish readers. Under the Mosaic law, the priesthood was limited to the tribe of Levi and the family of Aaron. And even those who were priests were forbidden to approach the Presence of God. Only the high priest could do that on one day of the year following the precisely ordained procedure outlined for the event by Jehovah.

In the new dispensation, all believers are priests with instant access to the Throne Room of the universe, day or night. Their function is to offer up spiritual sacrifices (in contrast to the animal, bird, and meal offerings of the Mosaic law). The spiritual sacrifices of the New Testament priest are:

1. The presentation of his body as a living sacrifice, holy and acceptable to God. This is an act of spiritual worship (Rom. 12:1).

2. The sacrifice of his praise. "That is, the fruit of lips that give thanks to His name" (Heb. 13:15).

3. The sacrifice of his good works. "Do not neglect doing good...." This sacrifice is pleasing to God (Heb. 13:16).

4. The sacrifice of his possessions, or his pocketbook. "Do not neglect ... sharing. ..." This sacrifice also is pleasing to the Lord (Heb. 13:16).

These sacrifices are acceptable to God through Jesus Christ. It is only through Christ, our Mediator, that we can approach God in the first place, and it is only He who can make our offerings acceptable to God. All that we do—our worship and our service—is imperfect, flawed by sin. But before it reaches the Father, it passes through the Lord Jesus. He removes all the sin, and when it reaches God the Father it is perfectly acceptable.

> To all our prayers and praises
> Christ adds His sweet perfume,
> And love the censer raises,
> These odors to consume.

The high priest in the Old Testament wore a gold plate on his turban with the words HOLY TO THE LORD (Ex. 28:36) written on it. It was for any sin that might be involved in the offerings of the people (Ex. 28:38). So our High Priest wears a miter for us, for any human failure that may be involved in our sacrifices.

> For us He wears the miter,
> Where holiness shines bright,
> For us His robes are whiter
> Than heaven's unsullied light.

The priesthood of all believers is a truth that should be understood, believed and joyfully practiced by every Christian. At the same time, it must not be abused. Though all believers are priests, not every priest has the right to preach or teach in the assembly. There are certain controls which must be observed.

    1. Women are forbidden to teach or to have authority over men; they are to keep silent (1 Tim. 2:12).

    2. Men who speak should do so as oracles of God (1 Pet. 4:11, KJV). That means they should have a distinct assurance that they are speaking the words which God would have them speak on that particular occasion.

    3. All believers have some gift, just as every member of the human body has some function (Rom. 12:6;

1 Cor. 12:7). But not all gifts involve public speaking. Not all have the special service gifts of evangelist, pastor or teacher (Eph. 4:11).

4. A young man should rekindle the gift of God that is within him (2 Tim. 1:6). If that gift involves preaching, teaching or some other form of public speaking, he should be given opportunity to exercise it in the assembly.

5. The priesthood of all believers is seen in operation in 1 Cor. 14:26:

What is *the outcome* then, brethren? When you assemble, each one has a psalm, has a teaching, has a revelation, has a tongue, has an interpretation. Let all things be done for edification.

In that same chapter are many controls limiting the public exercise of gifts in an assembly to insure order and edification. The universal priesthood of Christians must not be used to justify abuses in the local church.

2:6 Still thinking of the building, Peter reverts to Christ the Stone, and, in particular, to Christ as the Cornerstone. He shows that Christ's role as Cornerstone was foretold in Scripture, for he quotes from Isaiah 28:16. He points out that God has determined that Christ will have this unique position, that He is a chosen and precious Stone, and that He is completely dependable. No one who trusts in Him will ever be disappointed.

The cornerstone in this passage may be understood in at least three ways, and each applies with equal validity and force to the Lord Jesus.

1. A cornerstone in modern architecture is placed at the base of one corner, where it binds two walls together and symbolizes the foundation on which the entire building rests. Christ is the Cornerstone, the only genuine foundation (1 Cor. 3:10-11), the One who has

united believing Jews and Gentiles (like two walls in one building) into one new man (Eph. 2:13-14).

2. Some Bible students think that the cornerstone is the key stone in an arch. It is the stone which completes the arch and holds the rest of the building together. Our Lord certainly meets this description. He is the topmost stone in the arch, and without Him there would be no strength or cohesion to the building.

3. A third view is that the cornerstone is the top stone in a pyramid, occupying the highest place in the structure. It is the only stone in the structure of that shape. Its shape determines the shape of the entire pyramid. It is the last stone to be put in place. So Christ is the Capstone of the church, the truly unique Stone. The church gets its character from Him. When He returns, the building will be completed.

He is a Cornerstone *chosen* and *precious*. He is chosen in the sense that God has selected Him to occupy the place of chief honor. And He is precious because there is not another like Him.

"... He who believes in Him shall not be disappointed." The original passage in Isaiah from which this is quoted is rendered "... He who believes will not be in haste." Put these together and you have the wonderful promise that those who have Christ as their Cornerstone are saved from frustrating humiliation and from frantic haste.

2:7 In the preceding verses the Lord Jesus has been presented as the living Stone, a rejected Stone, a precious Stone and the Cornerstone. Now, without using the word, Peter seems to picture Him as the Touchstone. A touchstone reveals whether certain minerals rubbed against it are genuine or spurious. It shows, for instance, whether a nugget is gold or fool's gold.

When men come in contact with the Savior, they are

shown for what they really are. In their attitude toward Him they reveal themselves. To true believers, He is precious; unbelievers reject Him.

"To you who believe, he is precious" (RSV). The believer can get some small indication of how precious He is by trying to imagine what life would be without Him. Not all earthly pleasures are "worth comparing for a moment with a Christ-filled life." He is "distinguished among ten thousand. ... he is altogether desirable" (Song of Solomon 5:10, 16, RSV).

But what about those who do not believe? The writer of Psalm 118 predicted that this precious Stone would be rejected by the builders, but would later become the head of the corner. (Note that we are using the RSV here instead of the NASB.)

There is a persistent legend in connection with the building of Solomon's temple that perfectly illustrates this prophecy. The stones for the temple were prepared in advance in a nearby quarry. As they were needed they were raised up to the building site. One day the workers in the quarry sent up a stone of unique shape and proportions. The masons saw no place for it in the building so they carelessly pushed it over the hill where, in time, it became overgrown with moss and surrounded with weeds. As the temple neared completion, the masons called for a stone of certain dimensions. The men in the quarry replied, "We sent that stone up to you long ago." After careful search, the discarded stone was found and was set in its proper place in the temple.

The application is obvious. The Lord Jesus presented Himself to the nation of Israel at His first advent. But the people, and especially the rulers, had no room for Him in their scheme of things. They rejected Him and delivered Him up to be crucified.

But God raised Him from the dead and seated Him at His own right hand in heaven. When the Rejected One returns to earth the second time, He will come as King of kings and Lord of lords. He will then be publicly manifested as "head of the corner."

2:8 Now the figure changes from Christ the Touchstone and the Head of the corner to Christ the Stone of stumbling. Isaiah predicted that for those who did not believe, He would be a stone that will make men stumble and a rock that will make them fall (Isa. 8:14-15).

This was literally fulfilled in the history of the nation of Israel. When their Messiah came, the Jews were offended by His origins and His simple way of life. They wanted a political demagogue and a military strongman. In spite of the most convincing proofs, they refused to accept Him as the promised Messiah.

But this applies not only to Israel. For any who will not believe on Jesus, He becomes a stumbling stone and a rock that trips them. Men either bow before Him in repentance and faith to salvation or stumble over Him into hell. "What might have been their salvation is made the cause of their deeper condemnation." There can be no neutrality; He must be either Savior or Judge.

". . . For they stumble because they are disobedient to the world. . . ." Why do they stumble? Not because of honest intellectual difficulties. Not because there is anything about the Lord Jesus that makes it impossible to believe in Him. They stumble because they wilfully disobey the Word. The trouble is in the human will. The reason men are not saved is because they do not want to be saved (John 5:40).

The latter part of verse 8, "and to this doom they were also appointed," seems to say that they were destined to disobey the Word. Is this what it means? The answer is emphatically *no*. Nowhere does the Bible teach that God chooses men to be condemned. It is not His will that any should perish (2 Pet. 3:9). He desires all men to be saved and to come to the knowledge of the truth (1 Tim. 2:4).

What this verse does teach is that all those who wilfully disobey the Word are destined to stumble. The words "and to this doom they were also appointed" refer back to the entire preceding clause, "for they stumble because they are disobedient to the word." God has decreed that all who refuse to bow to the Lord Jesus will stumble. No one is foreordained to be disobedient, but if a man insists on going on in unbelief, then he is appointed to stumble. "Unwillingness to obey makes stumbling a foregone conclusion" (Phillips).

2:9 Peter turns again to the privileges of believers. They are a chosen race, a royal priesthood, a holy nation, God's own people. God had promised these very privileges to the nation of Israel if they would obey Him:

> Now then, if you will indeed obey My voice and keep My covenant, then you shall be My own possession among all the peoples, for all the earth is Mine; and you shall be to Me a kingdom of priests and a holy nation . . . (Ex. 19:5-6).

Because of unbelief Israel failed to realize the promise of God, and the nation forfeited its place as God's own people. During the present age, the church occupies the favored place that Israel lost through disobedience.

Believers today are a chosen race, chosen by God before the foundation of the world to belong to Christ (Eph. 1:4). But instead of being an earthly race with common ancestry and distinct physical characteristics, Christians are a heavenly people with divine parentage and spiritual resemblances.

Believers are also a royal priesthood. This is the second priesthood mentioned in this chapter. In verse 5 believers are described as holy priests, offering up spiritual sacrifices. Now they are said to be royal priests, proclaiming the excellencies of God. As holy priests, they enter the sanctuary of heaven by faith to worship. As royal priests, they go out into the world to witness. Wolston illustrates this difference in the priesthood by the imprisonment of Paul and Silas at Philippi. As holy priests they sang praises to God at midnight; as royal priests they preached the gospel to their jailor (Acts 16:25, 31).

Believers are a holy nation. It was God's intention that the people of Israel should be a nation distinguished by holiness. But the Israelites stooped to the sinful practices of their Gentile neighbors. So Israel has been set aside temporarily and the church is now God's holy nation.

Finally, Christians are a people for God's own possession. They belong to Him in a unique way and are of special value to Him.

The last part of verse 9 describes the responsibility of those who are God's new race, priesthood, nation and people. We should proclaim the excellencies of the One who called us out of darkness into His marvelous light. Once we were groping in the darkness of sin and shame. By a stupendous deliverance we have been translated into the kingdom of His dear Son. The light is as clear and brilliant as the darkness was oppressive. How we should shout the praises of the One who did all this for us!

2:10 Peter closes this section by referring to the book of the prophet Hosea. Using the prophet's own tragic family life as an object lesson, God had pronounced judgment on the nation of Israel. Because of their unfaithfulness to Him, He said that He would no longer have pity on them and that they would no more be His people (Hosea 1:6, 9). But the casting aside of Israel was not to be final, for the Lord also promised that in a future day, Israel would be restored:

> ... I will have mercy upon her that had not obtained mercy; and I will say to them which were not my people, Thou art my people; and they shall say, Thou art my God (Hosea 2:23, AV).

The people to whom Peter was writing had once been part of the nation of Israel. Now they were members of the church. Through faith in Christ, they had become the people of God, while unbelieving Jews were still cast aside.

So Peter sees in the condition of the converted Jews of his day a partial fulfillment of Hosea 2:23. In Christ, they had become God's new people; in Christ, they had received mercy. This handful of saved Jews enjoyed the blessings promised to Israel through Hosea long before Israel nationally would enjoy them.

No one should conclude from this passage in Peter that because the church is now God's people, He is through with Israel as a nation. Neither should one assume that the church is now the Israel of God, or that the promises made to Israel now apply to the church. Israel and the church are separate and distinct entities, and an understanding of this distinction is one of the most important keys in the interpretation of the prophetic Word.

Israel was God's chosen earthly people from the time of the call of Abraham to the coming of the Messiah. The nation's rebellion and faithlessness reached its awesome climax when Christ was nailed to the cross. Because of this crowning sin, God temporarily set aside Israel as His chosen people. They are His ancient earthly people today but not His chosen people.

During the present age, God has a new people—the church. This church age forms a parenthesis in God's dealings with Israel. When the parenthesis is closed, that is, when the church is caught away to heaven, God will resume His dealings with Israel. Then a believing portion of the nation will become God's people again.

The final fulfillment of Hosea's prophecy is still future. It will take place at the second advent. The nation that rejected its Messiah will "look on him whom they have pierced, they shall mourn for him, as one mourns for an only child, and weep bitterly over him, as one weeps over a first-born" (Zech. 12:10, RSV). Then repentant, believing Israel will receive mercy and will become God's people once more.

The point Peter is making in verse 10 is that believing Jews today enjoy an advance fulfillment of Hosea's prophecy, while unbelieving Jews are still alienated from God. The complete and final fulfillment will take place when "the Deliverer will come from Zion" and "banish ungodliness from Jacob" (Rom. 11:26, RSV).

V/The Christian Pilgrim And His Relation To The World (2:11-12)
    1/Personal Purity (v. 11):
    a/Relation To The World: *Beloved, I urge you as aliens and strangers*
    b/Response To Passions: *to abstain from fleshly lusts, which wage war against the soul.*
    2/Blameless Conduct (v. 12): *Keep your behavior excellent*
    a/Position: *among the Gentiles,*
    b/Accusation: *so that in the thing in which they slander you as evil-doers,*
    c/Demonstration: *they may on account of your good deeds, as they observe* them,
    d/Vindication: *glorify God in the day of visitation.*

2:11 Most of the rest of the epistle concerns the conduct that should characterize the Christian in the various relationships of life. Peter reminds believers that they are aliens and exiles in the world and that this fact should leave its stamp on all their behavior. They are aliens in the sense that they are living in a foreign country where they do not have the rights of citizens. They are exiles in the sense that they are obliged to live for a while in a place which is not their permanent home.

The hymns of yesterday remind us of our pilgrimage. For instance:

>Called from above, and heavenly men by birth
>(Who once were but the citizens of earth),
>As pilgrims here, we seek a heav'nly home,
>Our portion in the ages yet to come.

>We are but strangers here, we do not crave
>A home on earth, which gave Thee but a grave:
>Thy cross has severed ties which bound us here,
>Thyself our treasure in a brighter sphere.

But these sentiments have largely dropped from our hymnology. When the church has settled down in the world, it seems a bit hypocritical to be singing beyond our experience.

When we read the exhortation to "abstain from fleshly lusts, which wage war against the soul," we think immediately of sex sins. But the application is wider than that; it refers to any strong desire that is inconsistent with the will of God. It would include over-indulgence in food or drink, catering to the body with excessive sleep, the determination to amass material possessions, or the hankering for worldly pleasures. All these things wage incessant warfare against our spiritual well-being. They hinder communion with God. They deter spiritual growth.

2:12 Not only must we exercise discipline in the area of fleshly indulgence, but we must also maintain blameless conduct before the Gentiles, that is, the pagan world. In our day we must not pattern our lives after the world. We should be marching to the beat of a different drummer.

Almost inevitably we will be criticized. At the time Peter wrote this letter, the Christians "were being slandered as irreligious because not worshipping the heathen gods, as morons and ascetic because refraining from popular vices, as disloyal to the government because claiming allegiance to a heavenly King" (Erdman). Such criticism cannot be avoided. But under no circumstances should believers give the world a *valid* reason for such reproach. All slanders should be refuted by an unbroken record of good deeds. Then the accusers will be compelled to worship God on the day of visitation.

A day of visitation in the Bible means any time when the Lord draws near, either in grace or in judgment. The expression is used in Luke 19:41-44. Jesus wept over Jerusalem because it did not know the time of its visitation, that is, it did not realize that the Messiah had come in love and mercy. Here it may mean:

> 1. The day when God's grace will visit the critics and they are saved, or
>
> 2. the day of judgment when the unsaved will stand before God.

Saul of Tarsus illustrates the first interpretation. He had shared in accusing Stephen, but Stephen's good deeds triumphed over all opposition. When God visited Saul in mercy on the road to Damascus, the repentant Pharisee glorified God and went forth, like Stephen, to influence others by the radiance of a Christ-filled life. "The beautiful life is to raise men's thoughts in homage to the glorious God. When they behold the Divine realized in the human, they too are to be wooed into heavenly fellowship. They are to be wooed, not by the eloquence of our speech, but by the radiance of our behavior. By the imposing grace of noble living we are to 'put to silence the ignorance of foolish men,' and that silence will be for them the first stage in a life of aspiring consecration" (Jowett).

In the second interpretation, the thought is that unsaved people will be compelled to glorify God in the day of judgment. They will have no excuse, for they not only heard the gospel, they saw it in the lives of their Christian relatives, friends and neighbors. God will then be vindicated through the blameless conduct of His children.

VI/The Christian Citizen And His Relation To Government (2:13-17)
A/ Subjection (v. 13a): *Submit yourselves*
B/ Spirit (v. 13b): *for the Lord's sake*
C/ Sphere (v. 13c-14): *to every human institution:*
　1/Supreme Ruler (v. 13d): *whether to a king as the one in authority;*
　2/Subordinate Rulers (v. 14): *or to governors,*
　a/Power: *as sent by him*
　b/Punishment: *for the punishment of evil-doers*
　c/Praise: *and the praise of those who do right.*
D/ Strategy (vv. 15-17):
　1/Silencing The Opposition (v. 15): *For such is the will of God that by doing right you may silence the ignorance of foolish men.*
　2/Living In Liberty, Not Licence (v. 16): *Act as free men, and do not use your freedom as a covering for evil, but* use it *as bondslaves of God.*
　3/Giving Proper Respect to All (v. 17): *Honor all men; love the brotherhood, fear God, honor the king.*

2:13 The next five verses deal with the Christian's relation toward the government. The key word here is subjection. In fact, the injunction to submit is found four times in the epistle.
　Citizens are to be subject to the government (2:13).
　Slaves are to be subject to their masters (2:18).
　Wives are to be subject to their husbands (3:1).
　Younger believers are to be subject to the elder (5:5).
　"The ultimate Christian answer to persecutors, detractors and critics is that of a blameless life, conduct beyond reproach and good citizenship. In particular . . . submission is a supremely Christlike virtue" (Lyall).

Human governments are instituted by God (Rom. 13:1). Rulers are God's servants (Rom. 13:4). Even if the rulers are not believers, yet they are God's men officially. Even if they are dictators and tyrants, their rule is better than no rule at all. The complete absence of rule is anarchy, and no society can continue under anarchy. So any government is better than no government at all. Order is better than chaos.

Believers should submit to every human institution for the Lord's sake. In doing so, they are fulfilling His will and doing the thing that pleases Him.

These instructions apply to the emperor or to whoever is the supreme ruler. Even if Nero happens to be occupying the imperial palace, the general exhortation is to be subject to him.

2:14 The injunction of obedience applies to subordinate officials such as governors. They are authorized by God to punish offenders and to praise those who keep the law. Actually, government officials have little time or inclination to do the latter, but that does not alter the responsibility of the Christian to obey. Arnold Toynbee observed that "as long as original sin remains an element in human nature, Caesar will always have plenty to do."

Of course, there are exceptions. There is a time when obedience is not required. If a human government orders a believer to act contrary to the revealed will of God, then the believer must disobey the government. In that case he has a higher responsibility; he should obey God rather than men (Acts 5:29). If punishment is meted out for his disobedience, he should endure it courageously. Under no circumstances should he rebel or seek to overthrow the government.

Technically those who smuggle Bibles into closed countries are breaking the law. But they are obeying a law that has precedence over any human law—the command to go into all the world with the gospel. So they cannot be condemned on scriptural grounds.

Suppose the government orders a Christian into the armed forces. Is he obligated to obey and to bear arms? If he feels that this is in direct violation of God's Word, he should first exhaust any options that are open to him in the status of a non-combatant or a conscientious objector. If these fail, then he would have to refuse induction and bear the consequences.

Many Christians do not have conscientious scruples about serving in the military forces. It is a matter in which each one should be fully convinced in his own mind, and allow liberty for others to disagree.

The questions as to whether a Christian should vote or engage in politics are of a different order. The government does not demand these things, so it is not a question of obedience or disobedience. Each one must act in the light of the principles of conduct and citizenship found in the Bible. Here too we must allow liberty for differing viewpoints and not insist that others see eye to eye with us.

2:15   God's will is that His people should live so honorably and unblameably that the unconverted will have no legitimate basis for accusation. By lives of exemplary conduct, Christians can and should expose the ignorance of the charges made against Christianity unintelligent men.

Christians and the Christian faith are ceaselessly bombarded by the ignorance of foolish men. It may be in the university classroom; it may be in the science laboratory; it may be in the pulpit. Peter says that one of the best answers to such blasting is a holy life.

2:16   "Act as free men." We are not in bondage or slavery to civil authorities. We need not live in servility or terror. After all, we are the Lord's free men.

But that does not mean we are free to sin. Liberty does

not mean license. Freedom does not include lawlessness. So we must never use our freedom as a pretext for evil. Sinful disobedience should never be justified by some pseudo-spiritual excuse. The cause of Christ is never advanced by evil masquerading in religious clothes.

If we live as servants of God, our relationship with governmental authorities will fall into proper place. We are to act in the light of His presence, obey Him in all things, do all for His glory. The best citizen is a believer who lives as a bond-slave of the Lord. Unfortunately most governments don't realize how much they owe to Christians who believe and obey the Bible.

Ponder the expression *"bondslaves* of God." "Heaven takes our most dreaded terms, and makes them sparkle in its own light, till that which seemed the synonym of terror becomes the target of our noblest aims" (F. B. Meyer).

2:17 No relationship of life can be left outside the sphere of Christian responsibility. So Peter here runs the gamut with four crisp commands.

"Honor all men." We cannot always honor their words or their behavior. But we can remember that every single life is of more value than all the world. We can recognize that every person was made in the image and after the likeness of God. We must never forget that the Lord Jesus bled and died for even the most unworthy.

"Love the brotherhood." We are to love all men, but we are specially obligated to love the members of our spiritual family. This is a love like God's love for us. It is utterly undeserved, it goes out to the loveless, it looks for no reward, and it is stronger than death.

"Fear God." We fear Him when we reverence Him as the supreme Lord. Glorifying Him then becomes our number one priority. We fear doing anything that would displease Him and we fear misrepresenting Him before men.

"Honor the king." Peter returns to the subject of human rulers for a final reminder. We are to respect our rulers as officials appointed by God for the maintenance of an ordered society. This means we must pay "taxes to whom taxes are due, revenue to whom revenue is due, respect to whom respect is due" (Rom. 13:7, RSV). Generally speaking, the Christian can live under any form of government. The only time he should disobey is when he is ordered to compromise his loyalty or obedience to the Lord Jesus Christ.

VII/The Christian Servant And His Relation To His Master (2:18-25)

A/ The Basic Appeal (v. 18a): *Servants, be submissive to your masters*

B/ The Accompanying Attitude (v. 18b): *with all respect,*

C/ The Broad Application (v. 18c): *not only to those who are good and gentle, but also to those who are unreasonable.*

D/ The Divine Approval (vv. 19-20):
1/For Suffering Unjustly (v. 19): *For this* finds *favor, if for the sake of conscience toward God a man bears up under sorrows when suffering unjustly.*

2/Not For Deserved Punishment (v. 20a): *For what credit is it if, when you sin and are harshly treated, you endure it with patience?*

3/For Undeserved Suffering (v. 20b): *But if when you do what is right and suffer* for it *you patiently endure it, this* finds *favor with God.*

E/ The Unexpected Affirmation (v. 21a): *For you have been called for this purpose,*

F/ The Perfect Example (vv. 21b-24): *since Christ also suffered for you, leaving you an example for you to follow in His steps,*
1/Sinless (v. 22a): *who committed no sin,*
2/Guileless (v. 22b): *nor was any deceit found in his mouth;*

3/Patient (v. 23a): *and while being reviled, He did not revile in return;*
4/Gentle (v. 23b): *while suffering, He uttered no threats,*
5/Humble (v. 23c): *but kept entrusting* Himself *to Him who judges righteously;*
6/Sacrificial (vv. 24-25):
a/Person (v. 24a): *and He Himself*
b/Payment (v. 24b): *bore our sins*
c/Passion (v. 24c): *in His body*
d/Place (v. 24d): *on the cross,*
e/Purpose (v. 24e):
   [1] Death: *that we might die to sin*
   [2] Life: *and live to righteousness;*
f/Provision (vv. 24f-25): *for by His wounds you were healed.*
   [1] Past (v. 25a): *for you were continually straying like sheep,*
   [2] Present (v. 25b): *but now you have returned to the Shepherd and Guardian of your souls.*

2:18 It is significant that the New Testament gives more instructions to servants than to kings. Many of the early believers were servants, and the Scripture shows that most Christians came from the middle or lower strata of society (Matt. 11:5; Mk. 12:37, AV; 1 Cor. 1:26-29).

This passage is addressed to domestic servants but the principles apply to employees of any kind. The basic appeal is to submit to the master with all respect. It is a built-in fact of life that in any society or organization, there must be authority on the one hand, and obedience to that authority on the other. It is for any servant's own good to submit to his master, otherwise he would not have employment. But it is much more important for a *Christian* to submit. More than his pay check is involved; his testimony depends on it.

Obedience should not vary according to the temperament of the employer. Anyone can submit to an employer who is kind and gentle. Believers are called to go beyond that and be respectful and obedient to the overbearing boss. This stands out as distinctly Christian behavior.

2:19   When we suffer unjustly we win God's approval. He is pleased when He finds us so conscious of our relation to Him that we endure undeserved pain without vindicating self or fighting back. When we meekly take unjust treatment we display Christ; this supernatural life gains God's "Well done."

2:20   There is no virtue in suffering patiently for our own misdeeds. Certainly there is no glory for God in it. Such suffering will never mark us out as Christians, or make others want to become Christians.

But patient suffering for well-doing is the thing that counts. It is so unnatural, so other-worldly that it shocks people into conviction of sin and, hopefully, into salvation.

2:21   The thought of believers' suffering for righteousness' sake leads inevitably to this sublime passage on our great Example, the Lord Jesus. No one was ever treated as unjustly as He, or bore it as patiently.

We have been called to act as He acted, suffering for the wrongs of others. The word used here for *example* carries the idea of a copybook that contains flawless penmanship. The pupil seeks to reproduce the original as closely as possible. When he copies the model carefully, his writing is quite good. But the farther he moves away from it, the more the copy worsens. Our safety is in staying close to the Original.

2:22   It is obvious that our Lord did not suffer for His own sins for He had none. "He knew no sin" (2 Cor. 5:21); "He committed no sin" (here); "in Him there is no sin" (1 John 3:5).

His speech was never tainted by deceit. He never lied or even shaded the truth. Think about that! A Person once lived on this planet who was absolutely honest, absolutely free from trickery or deceit.

2:23 He was patient under provocation. When He was slandered He did not pay back in kind. When blamed He did not answer back. When accused He did not defend Himself. He was wondrously free from the lust of self-vindication.

"It is a mark of deepest and truest humility to see ourselves condemned without cause, and to be silent under it. To be silent under insult and wrong is a very noble imitation of our Lord. When we remember in how many ways He suffered, who in no way deserved it, where are our senses when we feel called to defend and excuse ourselves" (author unknown).

". . . While suffering, He uttered no threats. . . ." "No ungentle, threatening word escaped His silent Tongue." Perhaps His assailants mistook His silence for weakness. If they had tried it they would have found it was not weakness but supernatural strength.

What was His hidden resource in bearing up under such unprovoked abuse? He trusted God who judges justly. And we are called to do the same. "Beloved, never avenge yourselves, but leave it to the wrath of God; for it is written, 'Vengeance is mine, I will repay, says the Lord.' No, 'if your enemy is hungry, feed him; if he is thirsty, give him drink; for by so doing you will heap burning coals upon his head.' Do not be overcome by evil, but overcome evil with good" (Rom. 12:19-21, RSV).

2:24 The Savior's sufferings were not only exemplary, but expiatory as well. We cannot imitate His sufferings in this respect, and Peter does not suggest that we should. Rather the argument seems to be as follows: The Savior's agony was not brought on by His own sins for He had none. It was for our sins He was nailed to the cross. Because He has suffered for our sins once for all, we should never allow ourselves to get into the position where we have to suffer for them too. The fact that He died *for* them should cause us to die *to* them. And yet, it is not simply a matter of negative goodness; we should not only die to sin but live to righteousness.

". . . By His wounds you were healed." The word *wounds* is actually singular in the original, perhaps suggesting that His body was one massive welt. What should be our attitude toward sin when our healing cost the Savior so much? Theoderet comments, "A new and strange method of healing. The doctor suffered the cost, and the sick received the healing."

2:25 Before conversion, we were like straying sheep—lost, torn, bruised, bleeding. Peter's mention of straying sheep is the last of six references to Isaiah 53 in this passage:

v. 21 Christ . . . suffered for you (from Isa. 53:4-5).

v. 22 He committed no sin, nor was any deceit found in His mouth (from Isa. 53:9).

v. 23 Being reviled, He did not revile in return (from Isa. 53:7).

v. 24 He bore our sins in His body on the cross (from Isa. 53:4, 11).

v. 24 By His wounds you were healed (from Isa. 53:5).

v. 25 For you were continually straying like sheep (from Isa. 53:6).

When we are saved we return to the Shepherd—the good Shepherd who laid down His life for the sheep (John 10:11); the great **Shepherd** who "tends with sweet, unwearied care the flock for which He bled," and the Chief Shepherd who will soon appear to lead His sheep into the green pastures above from which they will never stray.

Conversion is returning to the Guardian of our souls. We were His by creation, but became lost through sin. Now we return to His keeping care, and are safe and secure for ever.

3

VIII/The Christian Wife And Her Relation To Her Husband (3:1-6)
A/ Subjection (vv. 1-2):
    1/Central Charge (v. 1a): *in the same way, you wives, be submissive*
    2/Specific Sphere (v. 1b): *to your own husbands*
    3/Extraordinary Evangelism (vv. 1c-2):
    a/The Word Disobeyed (v. 1c): *so that even if any of them are disobedient to the word*
    b/A Word Unnecessary (v. 1d): *they may be won without a word*
    c/The Word Displayed (vv. 1e-2): *by the behavior of their wives,*
        [1] Purity (v. 2a): *as they observe your chaste*
        [2] Respect (v. 2b): *and respectful behavior.*
B/ Adornment (vv. 3-4):
    1/The Artificial Avoided (v. 3): *and let not your adornment be external* only--*braiding the hair, and wearing gold jewelry, and putting on dresses;*
    2/The Appropriate Adopted (v. 4):
    a/Inward: *but* let it be *the hidden person of the heart,*
    b/Imperishable: *with the imperishable quality of a gentle and quiet spirit,*

c/Invaluable: *which is precious in the sight of God.*
C/ Adornment And Subjection (vv. 5-6):
1/Illustration (vv. 5-6a):
a/The Holy Women (v. 5): *For in this way in former times the holy women also, who hoped in God, used to adorn themselves, being submissive to their own husbands.*
b/Sarah (v. 6a): *Thus Sarah obeyed Abraham, calling him lord,*
2/Application (v. 6b): *and you have become her children*
a/Righteous Conduct: *if you do what is right*
b/Resulting Fearlessness: *without being frightened by any fear.*

3:1 The apostle Peter has stressed the obligation of Christians to submit to human government and to earthly masters. He now takes up the submission of wives to their husbands.

Every wife is to be submissive to her husband, whether he is a believer or not. God has given to the man the place of headship, and it is His will that the woman should acknowledge the authority of the man. The relationship between husband and wife is a picture of that between Christ and the church. The woman should obey her husband just as the church should obey Christ.

This is considered passe' in our society. Women are rising to places of authority over man, and our society is becoming increasingly matriarchal. In many churches, women seem to be more active and gifted than the men. But God's Word stands. The headship of man is the divine order. No matter how reasonable the arguments may sound, nothing but trouble and chaos can ultimately result when woman usurps authority over the man.

Even when a woman's husband is an unbeliever, she

should still respect him as her head. This will be a testimony to him of her faith in Christ. Her conduct as an obedient, loving, devoted wife may be used to win him to the Savior.

And she may win him "without a word." This means that the wife need not be preaching to her husband constantly. Possibly great harm has been done by wives who nagged their husbands concerning the gospel, forcing it down their throats. The emphasis here is on the wife's winning her husband by living Christ daily before him.

But suppose that a husband interferes with his wife in her Christian life. What should she do then? If he requires her to disobey a plain command of Scripture, then she must disobey her husband and be true to the Lord. If, however, the matter involves a Christian privilege rather than a clear duty, she should be subject to her husband and forego the privilege.

When Peter speaks about a Christian wife having a pagan husband, he does not thereby condone a believer's marrying an unbeliever. This is never God's will. The apostle is dealing primarily with cases where the wife was saved after marriage. Her obligation is to be submissive even to an unbelieving husband.

3:2 The unsaved husband may be impressed by the reverent and chaste behavior of his wife. The Spirit of God may use this to convict him of his own sinfulness, and he may come to faith in Christ.

George Müller told of a wealthy man in Germany whose wife was a devout believer. This man was a heavy drinker, spending late nights in the tavern. She would send the servants to bed, stay up till he returned, receive him kindly and never scold him or complain. At times she would even have to undress him and put him to bed.

One night in the tavern he said to his cronies, "I bet if we go to my house, my wife will be sitting up, waiting for me. She'll come to the door, give us a royal welcome and even make supper for us, if I ask her."

They were skeptical at first, but decided to go along and see.

Sure enough, she came to the door, received them courteously, and willingly agreed to make supper for them without the slightest trace of resentment.

After serving them, she went off to her room. As soon as she had left, one of the men began to condemn the husband. "What kind of a man are you to treat such a good woman so miserably?" The accuser got up without finishing his supper and left the house. Another did the same and another till they had all departed without eating the meal.

Within a half hour, the husband became deeply convicted of his wickedness, and especially of his heartless treatment of his wife. He went to his wife's room, asked her to pray for him, repented of his sins, and surrendered to Christ. From that time on, he became a devoted disciple of the Lord Jesus. Won without a word!

"Don't be discouraged if you have to suffer from unconverted relatives. Perhaps very shortly the Lord may give you the desire of your heart, and answer your prayer for them. But in the meantime, seek to commend the truth, not by reproaching them on account of their behavior toward *you*, but by manifesting toward *them* the meekness, gentleness and kindness of the Lord Jesus Christ" (George Müller).

3:3 The subject here seems to change to women's apparel, but actually the apostle is dealing primarily with the best ways for a wife to please and serve her husband. It is not her outward appearance that will influence him as much as her inner life of holiness and submission.

Various types of outward adorning are to be avoided:

    1. Braiding the hair. Some think that this excludes even modest braids. Others think that Peter is speaking

against the excess of mountainous coiffures with terraces of braids.

2. Wearing gold jewelry. Some interpret this as an absolute prohibition against any gold jewelry. Others see it as forbidding showy and extravagant displays.

3. Putting on dresses. Obviously it is not the wearing of clothing that is forbidden, but the wearing of ostentatious robes. Isaiah 3:16-25 tells what God thinks about all forms of extravagant adornment. Moreover, the Lord said, "Because the daughters of Zion are proud, And walk with heads held high and seductive eyes, And go along with mincing steps, And tinkle the bangles on their feet, Therefore the Lord will afflict the scalp of the daughters of Zion with scabs, And the Lord will make their foreheads bare. In that day the Lord will take away the beauty of their anklets, headbands, crescent ornaments, dangling earrings, bracelets, veils, headdresses, ankle chains, sashes, perfume boxes, amulets, finger rings, nose rings, festal robes, outer tunics, cloaks, money purses, hand mirrors, undergarments, turbans and veils. Now it will come about that instead of sweet perfume there will be putrefaction; Instead of a belt, a rope; Instead of well-set hair, a plucked-out scalp; Instead of fine clothes, a donning of sackcloth; And branding instead of beauty. Your men will fall by the sword, And your mighty ones in battle."

In the matter of clothing and jewelry, there are certain guidelines that apply to all believers, men as well as women.

A first principle is expense. How much do we spend on clothes? Is it all necessary? Could the money be spent in better ways?

1 Timothy 2:9 forbids expensive clothes: "not with. . . . costly garments." It is not a matter of whether or not we can afford them. It is sin for a Christian to spend money on expensive clothes, because God's Word forbids it.

Human compassion forbids it too. The desperate plight of our neighbors in other lands, their enormous spiritual and physical needs, point up the callousness of spending money unnecessarily on clothing.

This applies not only to the quality of the clothes we buy but to the quantity as well. The closets of some Christians look like branch clothing stores. Often as we travel on vacation, a rod stretched over the back seat of the car holds an array of dresses, shirts, and suits that rivals the samples of a traveling clothing salesman.

Why do we do it? Is it not a matter of pride? We love to be complimented on our good taste, our fine appearance. But another Voice says, "Your riches have rotted and your garments have become moth-eaten. Your gold and your silver have rusted; and their rust will be a witness against you and will consume your flesh like fire. It is in the Last Days that you have stored up your treasure! Behold, the pay of the laborers who mowed your fields, *and* which has been withheld by you, cries out *against you*; and the outcry of those who did the harvesting has reached the ears of the Lord of Sabaoth. You have lived luxuriously on the earth and led a life of wanton pleasure; you have fattened your hearts in a day of slaughter" (James 5:2-5).

The expense involved in buying clothes is only one principle that should guide us in its choice. Another is modesty. Paul says ". . . modestly and discreetly." One meaning of the word modest is "decent."

One of the functions of clothing is to hide man's nakedness. At least, that's the way it was in the beginning. But now clothing seems to be designed to reveal increasingly large areas of the anatomy. Man is thus glorying in his shame. It is not surprising to find ungodly men doing this, but it is rather shocking when Christians imitate them.

But modest can also mean orderly. This suggests that the Christian should dress neatly. There is no virtue in shabbiness, in untidiness. The believer's clothes should be clean, pressed, in good repair and well-fitting.

In general, the Christian must avoid fashions that attract attention to himself. That is not his function in life. He is not on earth as an ornament, but as a fruit-bearing branch of the Vine.

We can attract attention to ourselves in many ways. Wearing clothes that are old-fashioned will do it. The Christian should avoid wearing clothes that are uncommonly plain, or loud, or queer.

Finally, the Christian—and this may be a special problem for the young believer—should avoid clothes that are suggestive or provocative. We have already referred to fashions that are "revealing." But clothes can cover the whole body and still arouse unholy lust in others. Modern fashions are not designed to encourage spirituality. On the contrary they reflect the sex obsession of our age. The believer should never wear clothes that incite passions or make it hard for others to live a Christian life.

The great problem, of course, is the enormous social pressure to conform. This always has been true and always will be. Christians need plenty of spine to resist the extremes in fashion, to swim against the tide of public opinion, and to dress in a manner that befits the gospel.

If we make Christ the Lord of our wardrobe, all will be well.

3:4 The clothing which makes a believer genuinely attractive is the beauty of "the inner personality—the unfading loveliness of a calm and gentle spirit, a thing very precious in the eyes of God" (Phillips).

Fashionable coiffures, costly jewelry and fine clothing are perishable. The jewel of a gentle and quiet spirit is imperishable. In presenting this vivid contrast, Peter challenges us to make a choice. "There are plenty whose outward body is richly decked, but whose inner being is clothed in rags; while others whose garments are worn and threadbare are all glorious within" (F. B. Meyer).

Men think jewels are precious; God considers precious the jewel of a gentle and quiet spirit.

3:5 Godly women of the Old Testament adorned themselves by cultivating the moral and spiritual beauty of the inner life. One aspect of this beauty was a dutiful submission to their husbands.

These holy women hoped in God. They lived God-centered lives. Desiring to please Him in all things, they recognized His order in the home and were subject to their husbands.

3:6 Sarah is cited as an example. She obeyed Abraham, calling him lord. This takes us back to Genesis 18:12 (AV) where we read that Sarah said this "within herself." She did not go around and make a loud profession of submission to Abraham by publicly calling him *lord*. Rather in her inward life, she recognized him as her head, and this recognition was displayed by her actions.

Those women who follow Sarah's example are her children. The Jewish believers to whom Peter was writing were descendants of Sarah by natural birth. But to be her daughters or children in the best sense, they must imitate her personal character. Children should carry the family likeness.

They should do right and let nothing terrify them. This means that a Christian wife should fill her God-appointed role as an obedient helpmate, and not be terrified even if she must suffer the unreasonable, violent conduct of an unbelieving husband.

IX/The Christian Husband And His Relation To His Wife (3:7, RSV)

A/ Considerateness: *Likewise you husbands, live considerately with your wives,*
B/ Honor: *bestowing honor on the woman as the weaker sex,*
1/Privilege Asserted: *since you are joint heirs of the grace of life,*
2/Problem Averted: *in order that your prayers may not be hindered.*

3:7 Now the apostle turns to husbands and shows the corresponding duties which they must fulfill. They should live considerately with their wives, showing love, courtesy and understanding. They should bestow the tender regard on their wives that is appropriate for members of the weaker sex.

In this day of the women's liberation movement the Bible might seem out of step with the times in speaking of women as the "weaker sex." But it is a simple fact of life that the *average* woman is weaker than the man physically. Generally speaking, she does not have the same power to control her emotions and she is more frequently guided by emotional reactions than by rational, logical thought. The handling of deep theological problems is not characteristically her forte. And, in general, she is more dependent than the man.

But the fact that woman is weaker in some ways does not mean that she is inferior to man; the Bible never suggests this. Neither does it mean that she might not actually be stronger, or more competent in some areas. As a matter of fact, women are generally more devoted to Christ than men. And they are usually better able to bear prolonged pain and adversity.

A man's attitude toward his wife should recognize the fact that she is a fellow-heir of the grace of life. This refers, of course, to a marriage in which both are believers. Though weaker than the man in some ways, the woman enjoys equal standing before God and shares equally the gift of everlasting life.

When there is discord, prayers are hindered. It is very difficult for a couple to pray together when something is disrupting their fellowship. For the peace of the home and the welfare of its occupants it is important for husband and wife to observe a few basic rules.

    1. Maintain absolute honesty in order to have a basis of confidence between them.

    2. Keep lines of communication open. There must be a constant readiness to talk things out. When steam is allowed to build up in the boiler, an explosion is inevitable. Talking things out includes the willingness for each to say, "I am sorry" and to forgive—perhaps indefinitely.

    3. Overlook minor faults and idiosyncrasies. Love covers a multitude of sins. Don't demand perfection in others when you are unable to produce it in yourself.

    4. Strive for unity in finances. Avoid overspending, installment buying, and the lust to keep up with the Joneses.

    5. Remember that love is a commandment, not an uncontrollable emotion. Love means all that is included in 1 Cor. 13. Love is courteous, for instance; it will keep you from criticizing or contradicting your partner in front of guests. Love will keep you from quarreling in front of your children which could undermine their security. In these and a hundred other ways, love creates a happy atmosphere in the home and rules out strife and separations.

X/The Christian And His Relation To The Fellowship (3:8)
A/   Unity: *to sum up, let all be harmonious,*

B/ Sympathy: *sympathetic,*
C/ Brotherly Love: *brotherly,*
D/ Tenderheartedness: *kind-hearted,*
E/ Humility: *and humble in spirit;*

3:8 This verse deals primarily with the Christian and his relation to the fellowship. This seems evident from the exhortations to unity and to brotherly love. The other three exhortations could have a wider application, of course.

The words "To sum up" do not mean that Peter is about to close his epistle. He has been speaking to various classes of individuals such as servants, wives and husbands. Now, as a finale, he has a word for "all of you."

". . . Let all be harmonious." This means we are to be of one mind. It is not expected, however, that Christians will see eye-to-eye on everything. That would be uniformity, not unity. The best formula is contained in the well-known expression:

In fundamentals, unity
In non-essentials, liberty
In everything, love.

Then we are to have sympathy with one another. Literally, this means "to suffer with," and the admonition is especially appropriate when given, as it was, to those who were undergoing persecution. But the advice is for all times because no age is exempt from suffering.

". . . Brotherly." "Providence does not ask us whom we would like to be our brethren—that is settled for us; but we are bidden to love them, irrespective of our natural predilections and tastes. You say, 'That is impossible!' But remember that true love does not necessarily originate in the emotions, but in the will; it consists not in feeling but in doing; not in sentiment, but in action; not in soft words, but in noble and unselfish deeds" (Author Unknown).

". . . Kind-hearted." This is a heart that is sensitive to

the needs and feelings of others. It refuses to turn cold, callous or cynical in spite of the abuse it has to take.

"... And humble in spirit." Such was the mind of the Lord Jesus, as described in Phil. 2:5-8. The application to us is clearly stated: "Do nothing from selfishness or conceit, but in humility count others better than yourselves. Let each of you look not only to his own interests, but also to the interests of others" (Phil. 2:3-4, RSV).

XI/The Christian And His Relation To Persecutors (3:9—4:6)
A/ Orders Under Attack (3:9-12):
    1/Passive Endurance (v. 9*a*): *not returning evil for evil, or insult for insult,*
    2/Active Benevolence (v. 9*b*): *but giving a blessing instead;*
    a/Vocation (v. 9*c*): *for you were called for the very purpose*
    b/Benediction: (v. 9*d*): *that you might inherit a blessing.*
    c/Confirmation (vv. 10-12):
        [1] Desired Goals (v. 10*a*): For *"Let him who means to love life and see good days*
        [2] Definite Responsibilities (vv. 10*b*-11): *refrain his tongue from evil and his lips from speaking guile. And let him turn away from evil and do good; let him seek peace and pursue it.*
        [3] Divine Attitudes (v. 12): *"For the eyes of the Lord are upon the righteous, and his ears attend to their prayer, but the face of the Lord is against those who do evil."*
B/ A General Rule (3:13): *And who is there to harm you if you prove zealous for what is good?*
C/ A Possible Exception (3:14-16): *But even if you should suffer for the sake of righteousness,*
    1/Promised Blessing (v. 14*b*): you are *blessed.*

2/Fearless Behavior (v. 14c): *And do not fear their intimidation, and do not be troubled,*
3/Yielded Life (v. 15a): *but* sanctify *Christ as Lord in your hearts,*
4/Ready Response (v. 15b): *always being ready to make a defense to every one who asks you to give an account for the hope that is in you,*
a/Gentleness: *yet with gentleness*
b/Reverence: *and reverence;*
5/Clear Conscience (v. 16): *and keep a good conscience*
a/Slander: *so that in the thing in which you are slandered,*
b/Shame: *those who revile your good behavior in Christ may be put to shame.*

D/ A Definite Preference (3:17): *For it is better, if God should will it so, that you suffer for doing what is right rather than for doing what is wrong.*

E/ The Classic Example (3:18-22):
1/His Suffering (v. 18):
a/Expiation: *For Christ also died for sins*
b/Completion: *once for all,*
c/Substitution: the *just for* the *unjust,*
d/Reconciliation: *in order that He might bring us to God,*
e/Execution: *having been put to death in the flesh,*
f/Resurrection: *but made alive in the spirit;*
2/His Pre-incarnate Testimony (vv. 19-20):
a/Power (v. 19a): *in whom also*
b/Proclamation: (v. 19b): *He went and made proclamation*
c/Audience (v. 19c-20): *to the spirits*
  [1] Present Location (v. 19d): now *in prison,*
  [2] Past History (v. 20a):
    [a] Sin: *who once were disobedient,*
    [b] Time: *when the patience of God kept waiting in*

the days of Noah,

[c]   Duration: *during the construction of the ark,*

d/Result (v. 20*b*): *in which a few, that is, eight persons, were brought safely through* the *water.*

e/Analogy (vv. 21-22): *And corresponding to that,*

[1]   Salvation (v. 21*b*): *baptism now saves you—*

[2]   Explanation (v. 21*c*): *not the removal of dirt from the flesh, but an appeal to God for a good conscience—*

[3]   Foundation (v. 21*d*): *through the resurrection of Jesus Christ,*

[4]   Ascension (v. 22*a*, RSV): *who has gone into heaven*

[5]   Glorification (v. 22*b*, RSV): *and is at the right hand of God,*

[6]   Dominion (v. 22*c*, RSV): *with angels, authorities, and powers subject to him.*

3:9   This whole epistle is written against a backdrop of persecution and suffering. From this verse to 4:6 the subject is "The Christian and His Relation to Persecutors." Repeatedly, believers are urged to suffer for righteousness' sake without retaliating. We are not to repay evil for evil, or reviling for reviling. Instead we are to bless those who mistreat us, and to repay insult with kindness. As Christians, we are not called to harm others but to do them good, not to curse but to bless. Then God rewards this type of behavior with a blessing.

3:10   In the next three verses, Peter quotes Psalm 34:12-16*a* to confirm the fact that God's blessing rests on the man who refrains from evil deeds and evil speech and who practices righteousness.

The force of the first verse is this: The one who wishes to enjoy life to the hilt, and experience days of true happiness should refrain from speaking evil or deceit. In this section, of course, the thought is that he should not repay insult and lies in kind.

To love life is condemned in John 12:25; there it means to live for self and to disregard the true purpose of life. Here it means to live in the way God intended.

3:11 Not only evil speech, but evil deeds are forbidden. To retaliate only intensifies the conflict. It is stooping to use the world's weapons. The believer should repay evil with benevolence, and promote peace by meekly enduring abuse. Fire cannot be fought with fire.

> The only way to overcome evil is to let it run its course, so that it does not find the resistance it is looking for. Resistance merely creates further evil and adds fuel to the flames. But when evil meets no opposition and encounters no obstacle but only patient endurance, its sting is drawn, and at last it meets an opponent which is more than its match. Of course this can only happen when the last ounce of resistance is abandoned, and the renunciation of revenge is complete. Then evil cannot find its mark, it can breed no further evil, and is left barren (Selected).

3:12 The Lord looks with approval on those who act righteously. He is attentive to their prayers. Of course, the Lord hears the prayers of all His people. But He undertakes in a special sense the cause of those who suffer for Christ's sake without returning evil for evil.

"The face of the Lord is against those who do evil." This primarily refers to the persecutors of His people. But it may also include the believer who fights back against his foes with physical violence and intemperate language. Evil is evil, and God opposes it wherever He finds it—whether in the saved or in the lost.

In quoting Psalm 34:16, Peter left out the closing

words: ". . . to cut off the memory of them from the earth." This omission was not an oversight. We are living in the dispensation of the grace of God; it is the acceptable year of the Lord. The day of vengeance of our God has not come as yet. When the Lord Jesus returns as King of kings and Lord of lords, He will punish evildoers and cut off the memory of them from the earth.

3:13 Peter resumes his argument with a question. "And who is there to harm you if you prove zealous for what is good?" The answer implied is "No one." And yet the history of the martyrs seems to prove that enemies of the gospel do harm faithful disciples.

There are at least two possible explanations of this paradox:

> 1. Generally speaking, those who follow a path of righteousness are not harmed. A policy of nonresistance disarms the opposition. There may be exceptions, but as a rule, the one who is eager for the right is protected from harm by his very goodness.
>
> 2. The worst that the foe can do to a Christian does not give eternal harm. The enemy can injure his body but he cannot damage his soul.

During the last war a Christian boy of twelve refused to join a certain movement in Europe.

"Don't you know that we have power to kill you?" they said.

"Don't you know," he replied quietly, "that I have power to die for Christ!"

He had the conviction that no one was able to harm him.

3:14 But suppose a Christian does suffer persecution because of his loyalty to the Savior! What then? Three results follow:

1. God overrules the suffering for His own glory.
2. He uses the suffering to bring blessing to others.
3. He blesses the one who suffers for His name.

"And do not fear their intimidation, and do not be troubled." Don't be afraid of men, or terrified by their threats. How well the martyrs lived out this policy! When Polycarp was promised release if he would blaspheme Christ, he said, "Eighty and six years have I served Christ and He has never done me wrong: how can I blaspheme my King and my Savior?" When the proconsul threatened to expose him to the wild beasts, he replied, " 'Tis well for me to be speedily released from this life of misery." Finally the ruler threatened to burn him alive. Polycarp said, "I fear not the fire that burns for a moment: Thou knowest not that which burns for ever and ever."

3:15 In the last part of verse 14 and in this verse, Peter quotes from Isaiah 8:12*b*-13.

> And you are not to fear what they fear or be in dread of it. "It is the Lord of hosts whom you should regard as holy. And He shall be your fear, And He shall be your dread."

Someone has said, "We fear God so little because we fear man so much."

The Isaiah passage speaks of *The Lord of hosts* as the One to be reverenced. Quoting it, Peter, by inspiration of the Holy Spirit, says, "reverence *Christ as Lord*." What can this mean but that the Lord of hosts is Jesus Christ? Jehovah Sabaoth of the Old Testament is the Lord Jesus of the New Testament.

To reverence Christ as Lord means to make Him the Sovereign of our lives. All we do and say should be in His will, for His pleasure, and for His glory. The Lordship of Christ should dominate every area of our lives—our possessions, our occupation, our library, our marriage, our spare glory.

Notice the six features of His sufferings:

1. They were expiatory, that is, they freed believing sinners from the punishment of their sins.

2. They were everlastingly effectual. He died once for all and settled the sin question. The work of redemption was completed.

3. They were substitutionary. The just died for the unjust. "The Lord has caused the iniquity of us all to fall on Him" (Isa. 53:6*b*).

4. They were reconciling. Through His death we have been brought to God. The sin which caused alienation has been removed.

5. They were violent. His death was by execution.

6. Finally, they were climaxed by resurrection. He was raised from the dead on the third day.

The expression "made alive in the spirit," has two principle interpretations. One is that He was made alive in His own human spirit. The other is that He was raised by the Holy Spirit. We must remember that His spirit never died; it was His body that died. We favor the second view—that His resurrection was through the power of the Holy Spirit.

3:19 The passage now before us (vv. 19-20) is easily one of the most puzzling and intriguing in the New Testament. It has been made the pretext for such unbiblical doctrines as purgatory on the one hand and universal salvation on the other. However, among evangelical Christians, there are two commonly accepted interpretations.

According to the first, Christ went to Hades in spirit between His death and resurrection, and proclaimed the triumph of His mighty work on the cross. There is disagreement among proponents of this view as to whether "the spirits in prison" were believers, unbelievers, or both. But there is fairly general agreement that the Lord Jesus did not time—nothing can be excluded.

"Always being ready to make a defense to every one who asks you to give an account for the hope that is in you, yet with gentleness and reverence." This applies primarily to times when Christians are being persecuted because of their faith. The consciousness of the presence of the Lord Christ should impart a holy boldness and inspire the believer to witness a good confession.

Of course, the verse is also applicable to everyday life. People often ask us questions which quite naturally open the door to speak to them about the Lord. We should be ready to tell them what great things the Lord has done for us.

This witnessing should be done in either case with gentleness and reverence. There should be no trace of harshness, bitterness or flippancy when we speak of the Lord Jesus, our Savior and Lord.

3:16 The believer must have a good conscience. If he knows he is innocent of any crime, he can go through persecution with the boldness of a lion. If he has a bad conscience, he will be plagued with feelings of guilt and will not be able to stand against the foe.

Even if a believer's life is blameless, the enemies of the gospel will still find fault with him and bring false charges against him. But when the case comes to trial, and the charges are found to be empty, the accusers are put to shame.

3:17 If a Christian must suffer, it should be for well-doing, which might sometimes be God's will for him. But he should not bring suffering upon himself for his own misdeeds; there is no virtue in that.

3:18 The remainder of the chapter presents Christ as the classic example of One who suffered for righteousness' sake, and reminds us that for Him, suffering was the pathway to preach the gospel to them. That would involve the doctrine of a second chance which is nowhere taught in the Bible. Those who hold this view often link this passage with Eph. 4:9 where the Lord is described as descending "into the lower parts of the earth." They cite this as added proof that He went to Hades in the disembodied state and heralded His victory at Calvary.

The second interpretation is that Peter is describing what happened in the days of Noah. It was the spirit of Christ who preached through Noah to the unbelieving generation before the flood. They were not disembodied spirits at that time, but living men and women who rejected the warnings of Noah and were destroyed by the flood. So *now* they are spirits in the prison of Hades.

This second view is the one that best fits the context and has the least difficulties connected with it. Let us examine the passage phrase by phrase.

"In whom also He went and made proclamation to the spirits *now* in prison." The relative pronoun "whom" obviously refers back to "spirit" at the end of v. 18. We understand this to mean the Holy Spirit. In 1:11 of this letter the Spirit of Christ, that is, the Holy Spirit, is described as speaking through the prophets of the Old Testament. And in Gen. 6:3 God speaks of His Spirit, that is, the Holy Spirit, as nearing the limit of endurance with the ante-diluvians.

"He went and made proclamation." As already mentioned, it was Christ who preached but He preached through Noah. In 2 Peter 2:5 Noah is described as "a herald of righteousness" (RSV). It is the same root word used of Christ's preaching—"he went and heralded."

"To the spirits *now* in prison." These were the people to whom Noah preached—living men and women who heard the warning of an impending flood and of salvation in the ark. They rejected the message and were drowned in the deluge. They are now disembodied spirits in prison, awaiting the final judgment.

So the verse may be amplified as follows: "in whom (the Holy Spirit) He (Christ) went and made proclamation (through Noah) to the spirits *now* in prison (Hades)."

But what right do we have to assume that the spirits in prison were the living men in Noah's day? The answer is found in the following verse.

3:20   Here the spirits in prison are unmistakably identified.
Who were they?
Those "who once were disobedient . . ."

When were they disobedient?
". . . when the patience of God kept waiting in the
days of Noah, during the construction of the ark . . ."

What was the final outcome?
Only "a few, that is, eight persons, were brought
safely through *the* water."

It is well to pause here and remind ourselves of the general flow of thought in this letter which was written against a general background of persecution. The Christians to whom Peter wrote were suffering because of their life and testimony. Perhaps they wondered why, if the Christian faith was right, they should be suffering rather than reigning. If Christianity was the true faith, why were there so few Christians.

To answer the first question, Peter points to the Lord Jesus. Christ suffered for righteousness' sake, even to the extent of being put to death. But God raised Him from the dead and glorified Him in heaven (see v. 22). The pathway to glory led through the valley of suffering.

Next Peter refers to Noah. For 120 years this faithful preacher warned that God was going to destroy the world with water. His thanks was scorn and rejection. But God vindicated him by saving him and his family through the flood.

Then there is the problem, "If we are right, why are there so few of us?" Peter answers: "There was a time when only eight people in the world were right and all the rest were wrong." Characteristically in the world's history the majority has not been right. True believers are usually a small remnant, so one's faith should not falter because of the small number of the saved. There were only eight believers in Noah's day; there are thousands upon thousands today.

But now to go back to the text. At the end of v. 20, we read that "a few, that is, eight persons, were brought safely through *the* water." It is not that they were saved *by* water; they were saved *through* the water. Water was not the savior, but the judgment through which God brought them safely.

To properly understand this statement and the verse that follows, we must see the typical meaning of the ark and of the flood. The ark is a picture of the Lord Jesus Christ. The flood of water depicts the judgment of God. The ark was the only way of salvation. When the flood came, only those who were inside were saved; all those on the outside perished. So Christ is the only way of salvation; those who are in Christ are as saved as God Himself can make them. Those on the outside could not be more lost.

The water was not the means of salvation, for all who were in the water drowned. The ark was the place of refuge. The ark went through the water of judgment; it took the full brunt of the storm. Not a drop of water reached those who were inside the ark. So Christ bore the fury of God's judgment against our sins. For those who are in Him there is no judgment (John 5:24).

The ark had water beneath it and water coming down on top of it, water all around. But it bore its believing occupants *through* the water to safety in a renewed creation. So those who trust the Savior are brought safely through a scene of death and desolation to resurrection ground.

3:21 "And corresponding to that, baptism now saves you..." Once again we are in difficult and controversial territory. This verse has been a battleground between those who teach baptismal regeneration and those who deny that baptism has any power to save.

First let us see what it may mean, and then what it cannot mean.

Actually there is a baptism which saves us—not our baptism in water, but a baptism which took place at Calvary almost 2000 years ago. Christ's death was a baptism. He was baptized in the waters of judgment. This is what He meant when He said, "I have a baptism to undergo, and how distressed I am until it is accomplished!" (Luke 12:50). The psalmist described this baptism in the words, "Deep calls unto deep at the sound of Thy waterfalls: All Thy breakers and Thy waves have rolled over me" (Psalm 42:7). In His death, Christ was baptized in the waves and billows of God's wrath, and it is this baptism that is the basis for our salvation.

But we must accept His death for ourselves. Just as Noah and his family had to enter the ark to be saved, so we must commit ourselves to Him as our only Lord and Savior. When we do this, we become identified with Him in His death, burial and resurrection. In a very real sense, we then have been crucified with Him (Gal. 2:20), we have been buried with Him (Rom. 6:4), and we have been brought from death to life with Him (Rom. 6:4).

All this is pictured in the believer's baptism. The ceremony is an outward sign of what has taken place spiritually; we have been baptized into Christ's death. As we go under the water, we acknowledge that we have been buried with Him. As we come up out of the water, we show that we have risen with Him and want to walk in newness of life.

"Baptism now saves you..." refers to Christ's baptism

unto death on the cross and our identification with Him in it, which water baptism represents.

The verse cannot mean that we are saved by ritual baptism, for the following reasons:

    1. That would make water the savior, instead of the Lord Jesus. But He said, "I am the way" (John 14:6).

    2. It would imply that Christ died in vain. If people can be saved by water, then why did the Lord Jesus have to die?

    3. It simply doesn't work. Many who have been baptized have proved by their subsequent lives that they were never truly born again.

Neither can the verse mean that we are saved by *faith plus baptism*.

    1. This would mean that the Savior's work on the cross was not sufficient. When He cried, "It is finished," it wasn't really so, according to this view, because baptism must be added to that work for salvation.

    2. If baptism is necessary for salvation, it is strange that the Lord did not personally baptize anyone. John 4:1-2 states that Jesus did not do the actual baptizing of His followers; this was done by His disciples.

    3. The Apostle Paul thanked God that he baptized very few of the Corinthians (1 Cor. 1:14-16). This would be strange thanksgiving for an evangelist if baptism were essential for salvation. The fact that Paul did baptize some shows that he taught believer's baptism, but the fact that he baptized only a few shows that he did not consider it a requirement for salvation.

    4. The penitent thief on the cross was not baptized, yet he was assured of being in Paradise with Christ (Luke 23:43).

    5. The Gentiles who were saved in Caesarea (Acts 10:44) received the Holy Spirit when they believed,

showing that they then belonged to Christ (Rom. 8:9b). After receiving the Holy Spirit, that is, after being saved, they were baptized (vv. 47-48). Therefore, baptism was not necessary for their salvation. They were saved first, then baptized.

6. In the New Testament baptism is always connected with death and not with spiritual birth.

7. There are about 150 passages in the New Testament which teach that salvation is by faith alone. These cannot be contradicted by two or three verses that *seem* to teach that baptism is necessary for salvation.

Therefore when we read in v. 21, "Baptism now saves you," it does not mean our baptism in literal water, but Christ's baptism unto death and our identification with Him in it.

The text continues, "not the removal of dirt from the flesh...." The ceremonial worship of the Old Testament, with which Peter's Jewish-Christian readers were familiar, provided a sort of external cleansing. But it was not able to give the priests or the people a clear conscience with regard to sin.

The baptism of which Peter is speaking is not a question of physical or even of ritual cleansing from defilement. Water does have the effect of removing dirt from the body, but it cannot provide a good conscience toward God. Only personal association with Christ in His death, burial and resurrection can do that.

Peter goes on: "... but an appeal to God for a good conscience—through the resurrection of Jesus Christ...." The question inevitably arises, "How can I have a righteous standing before God? How can I have a clear conscience before Him?" The answer is found in the baptism of which Peter has been speaking—Christ's baptism unto death at Calvary and one's personal acceptance of that work. By Christ's death the sin question was settled once for all.

How do I know that God is satisfied? I know because He raised Christ from the dead. A clear conscience is inseparably linked with the resurrection of Jesus Christ; they stand or fall together. The resurrection tells me that God is fully satisfied with the redemptive work of His Son. If Christ had not risen, we could never be sure that our sins had been put away. He would have died like any other man. But the risen Christ is our absolute assurance that the claims of God against our sins have been fully met.

"Our conscience has peace that can never fail: 'tis the Lamb on high, on the throne."

So "baptism now saves you . . . an appeal to God for a good conscience, through the resurrection of Jesus Christ." My only claim for a good conscience is based on the death, burial and resurrection of the Lord Jesus. The order is as follows:

1. Christ was baptized unto death for me at Calvary.

2. When I trust Him as Lord and Savior, I am spiritually united with Him in His death, burial and resurrection.

3. Through the knowledge that He has risen, my request for a clear conscience is answered.

4. In water baptism, I give visible expression to the spiritual deliverance I have experienced.

3:22 "Who has gone into heaven and is at the right hand of God, with angels, authorities, and powers subject to him" (RSV).

The Lord Jesus Christ not only arose from among the dead, but He ascended to heaven from where He had originally come. He is there today, not as an invisible, intangible spirit-being, but as a living Man in a glorified body of flesh and bones. In that body He bears eternally the wounds He received at Calvary—eloquent and everlasting tokens of His love for us.

> Arisen, radiant from the dead,
> Thy sorrow's scars forever tell,
> Creation's Head is He who bled—
> Still Jesus, still Immanuel.

Our Lord is at the right hand of God. The right hand is the place of:

Power: Since the right hand is generally stronger than the left, it has come to be associated with power (Matt. 26:64).

Honor: Christ is "*exalted* to the right hand of God" (Acts 2:33; 5:31).

Rest: In virtue of His finished work Christ "*sat down* at the right hand of the Majesty on high" (Heb. 1:3; see also 8:1; 10:12). This rest, of course, is the rest of satisfaction and completion, not the rest that conquers weariness.

Intercession: Paul speaks of Christ being at the right hand of God where He *intercedes* for us (Rom. 8:34).

Pre-eminence: At the right hand of God "in the heavenly *places*, (He is) *far above all* rule and authority and power and dominion, and every name that is named, not only in this age, but also in the one to come . . ." (Eph. 1:20-21).

Dominion: In Heb. 1:13, God the Father says to the Son, "Sit at my right hand, *until I make thine enemies a footstool for thy feet.*" The thought of dominion is emphasized in 1 Peter 3:22: ". . . at the right hand of God, with angels, authorities and powers subject to Him" (RSV).

Angels, authorities and powers are doubtless intended to cover all ranks of heavenly beings. They are all servants of the risen, glorified Christ.

This then was our Lord's experience in suffering for well-doing. Men rejected Him, both in His pre-incarnate testimony through Noah and in His first advent as the Son of Man. He was baptized in death's dark waters at Calvary. But God raised Him from the dead and glorified Him at His own right hand in heaven. In the eternal purposes of God, the sufferings had to precede the glory.

This was the lesson for Peter's readers and is the lesson for us. We should not be upset if we suffer affliction and persecution for doing good, for we do not deserve better treatment than our Savior had when He was on earth. We should comfort ourselves with the promise that if we suffer with Him, we shall be glorified with Him (Rom. 8:17). What is more, the sufferings now are not worthy to be compared with the glory that awaits us (Rom. 8:18). The afflictions are slight and momentary; the glory is eternal and weighty beyond all comparison (2 Cor. 4:17).

4

XI/The Christian And His Relation To Persecutors (3:9—4:6) (Cont'd.)

F/ The Practical Application (4:1-6):

1/A Pattern To Imitate (v. 1a): *Therefore, since Christ has suffered in the flesh,*

2/A Call To Follow (v. 1b): *arm yourselves also with the same purpose,*

3/A Freedom To Enjoy (v. 1c): *because he who has suffered in the flesh has ceased from sin,*

4/A Life To Live (v. 2): *so as to live the rest of the time in the flesh no longer for the lusts of men, but for the will of God.*

5/A Past To Repudiate (vv. 3-5): *For the time already past is sufficient* for you

a/The Gentiles' Behavior (v. 3b): *to have carried out the desire of the Gentiles,*

b/Their Sins (v. 3c): *having pursued a course of sensuality, lusts, drunkenness. carousals, drinking parties and abominable idolatries.*

c/Their Surprise (v. 4a): *And in* all *this, they are surprised that you do not run with* them *into the same excess of dissipation,*

d/Their Slander (v. 4b): *and they malign you;*

e/Their Judgment (v. 5): *but they shall give account to Him who is ready to judge the living and the dead.*
6/An Encouragement To Remember (v. 6):
a/God's Proclamation: *For the gospel has for this purpose been preached even to those who are dead,*
b/Man's Condemnation: *that though they are judged in the flesh as men,*
c/God's Vindication: *they may live in the spirit according to the* will of *God.*

4:1 There is a close connection between this section and the preceding (compare this verse with 3:18). We have been considering Christ as an example of One who suffered unjustly. He suffered at the hands of wicked men for the cause of righteousness. Since this is so, His followers should arm themselves with the same thought. They should expect to suffer for His Name. They should be prepared to endure persecution because they are Christians.

Whoever has "suffered in the flesh," that is, in the body, "has ceased from sin." The believer is faced with two possibilities—sin or suffering. On the one hand, he can choose to live like the unsaved people around him, sharing their sinful pleasures, and thus avoid persecution. Or he can live in purity and godliness, bearing the reproach of Christ, and suffer at the hands of the wicked.

When a believer deliberately chooses to suffer persecution as a Christian rather than to continue in a life of sin, he has "ceased from sin." This does not mean that he no longer commits acts of sin, but that the power of sin in his life has been broken. When a man suffers because he refuses to sin, he is no longer controlled by the will of the flesh.

4:2 The expression "ceased from sin" means that during the remainder of a believer's earthly life, he is not controlled by human passions but by the will of God. He prefers to suffer as a Christian rather than to sin like the unbelievers. He would rather die than deny his Lord.

The words "the rest of the time in the flesh" mean the remainder of his life here on earth. The believer chooses to live these years for the glory of God rather than for the gratification of sensual appetites.

4:3 Peter is writing to those who were Jews before their conversion, who had at times committed the same sins for which the Gentiles were notorious. According to Peter, there had been enough of that kind of life. As Christians, they were new creatures, and the old sins should be abandoned. The remaining years of life belonged to God and should be given to Him.

The sins listed are those that characterize the Gentile non-Christian world today—the sins of sex, of liquor and of false religion.

Sensuality—unrestrained indulgence, primarily in sexual immorality.

Lust—gratification of unlawful appetites of any kind, but probably referring especially to sins of sex.

Drunkenness—giving oneself over to the control of intoxicating beverages with the resulting weakening of will-power to resist temptation. There is a close link between drunkenness and immorality.

Carousals—riotous parties and late-night merry-making.

Drinking parties—drinking bouts which lead to debauchery and brawls.

Abominable idolatries—the worship of idols, with all the immorality that is associated with such worship. Men become like what they worship. When they abandon the true God, their moral standards are automatically lowered. These lowered standards permit them to engage in all sorts of sinful pleasures for which they have an appetite.

This is why idolatrous religions breed sin and degradation.

4:4 This verse describes the common experience of those who are saved from lives of outward corruption. Their former cronies think they have gone mad and accuse them of being religious fanatics. They think it a form of insanity that the Christians will no longer participate in dances, parties and sex orgies.

> Lions and beasts of savage name
> Put on the nature of the lamb,
> While the wide world esteems it strange,
> Gaze, and admire, and hate the change.

The clean, moral life of a believer condemns the sinner; no wonder he hates the change.

4:5 Though the ungodly blaspheme Christians in this life, they will give an account for every word and deed at the judgment of the Great White Throne. The Lord is prepared to judge the living and the dead. Clearly it is unbelievers whom Peter has in mind here. The judgment of living unbelievers will take place before the millennium begins; the wicked dead will be judged at the close of Christ's reign on earth. Their condemnation will be proof of the righteousness of the children of God.

4:6 It is for this purpose—the vindication of the children of God—that the gospel was preached to those who are dead. Here again we come to a difficult passage. Does this mean that the gospel was preached to people after they had died or while they were still alive? And who were these people?

We understand this verse to refer to all the people to whom the gospel was preached while they were still alive on the earth and who believed on the Lord. Because of their valiant stand for the truth they suffered at the hands of wicked men, and in some cases were martyred. These believers, though judged, or condemned, according to men in the flesh, were vindicated by God. They are now enjoying eternal life with Him.

They were not dead when the gospel was preached to them. But they are dead now, as far as their bodies are concerned. Though men thought them mad, God honored them, and their spirits are now in heaven.

The preaching of the gospel brings two results to those who believe—the blame of men and the approval of God. "The design in publishing the Gospel to them was, that though they might be judged by men in the usual manner, and put to death, yet that in respect to their higher and nobler nature, *the spirit*, they might live unto God" (Barnes).

XII/Urgent Imperatives For The Last Days (4:7-11): The end of all things is at hand;
A/ Unruffled Prayer (v. 7b): *therefore, be of sound judgment and sober* spirit *for the purpose of prayer.*
B/ Unfailing Love (v. 8): *Above all, keep fervent in your love for one another, because love covers a multitude of sins.*
C/ Ungrudging Hospitality (v.9): *Be hospitable to one another without complaint.*
D/ Unselfish Service (vv. 10-11):
1/The General Principle (v. 10):
a/Individual Gifts (v. 10a): *As each one has received a special gift,*
b/Mutual Benefit (v. 10b): *employ it in serving one another,*
c/Sacred Responsibility (v. 10c): *as good stewards of the manifold grace of God.*
2/The Specific Applications (v. 11a-b):
a/Speaking (v. 11a): *Whoever speaks,* let him speak; *as it were, the utterances of God;*
b/Service (v. 11b): *whoever serves,* let him do so *as by*

the strength which God supplies;
3/The Glorious Goal (v. 11c): *so that in all things God may be glorified through Jesus Christ,*
4/The Fitting Doxology (v. 11d): *to whom belongs the glory and dominion forever and ever. Amen.*

4:7 A series of admonitions is now introduced by the statement, "The end of all things is at hand." This has been taken to mean either (1) the destruction of Jerusalem, (2) the rapture, (3) the return of Christ to reign, or (4) the destruction of the heavens and the earth at the end of the millennium. We think it probably refers to the last of these.

The first admonition is ". . . be of sound judgment and sober *spirit* for the purpose of prayer." This was written in a time of persecution and means that the believer's prayer life should be free from the distractions of panic and of emotional instability brought on by stress: His fellowship with God should be undisturbed by discordant circumstances.

4:8 He must pay attention to his fellowship with other believers (vv. 8-9), and have unfailing love for all members of the household of faith. Such a love will not publicize the faults and failings of other believers, but will protect them from public view. Someone has said, "Hatred makes the worst of everything. Love is entitled to bury things out of sight."

The statement that "love covers a multitude of sins" should not be taken as a doctrinal explanation of how sins are put away. The guilt and penalty of sins can only be removed by the blood of Christ. Neither should the statement be used to condone sin or to relieve an assembly from its responsibility to discipline an offender. It means that true love is able to overlook minor faults and failures in other believers.

4:9 One means of demonstrating love to the brethren is by practicing hospitality ungrudgingly. This counsel is especially needed during times of persecution when food supplies might be running low and when those who harbor Christians are subject to arrest and imprisonment, if not death itself.

Hospitality is a tremendous privilege. In practicing it, some have entertained angels unawares (Heb. 13:2, AV). Any kindness shown to a child of God is reckoned as shown to the Lord Himself (Matt. 25:40). No matter how slight the kindness, it will be rewarded handsomely; even a cup of cold water given in the Lord's name will be rewarded (Matt. 10:42). Those who receive a prophet because he is a prophet shall receive a prophet's reward (Matt. 10:41) which, in Jewish reckoning, was superlative. Many Christians testify to the blessing that has come to their homes and their children through hospitality shown to servants of the Lord.

Jesus taught that we should entertain those who cannot repay us (Luke 14:12). This does not mean that we should *never* entertain relatives, friends or neighbors who might entertain us in return. But our purpose should be to show kindness in the name of the Lord Jesus with no thought of being repaid. Certainly it is questionable whether believers should keep up a continuing round of banquets and parties, with their own clique, while great sections of the world are still unevangelized.

4:10 Each believer has received a gift from the Lord, some special function to perform as a member of the body of Christ (1 Cor. 12:4-11, 29-31; Rom. 12:6-8). These gifts are a stewardship from God. They are not to be used for selfish gain but for His glory and for the good of others. We are not meant to be the final terminals of God's gifts to us. His grace reaches us but should not end with us. We are intended to be channels through whom the blessings can flow to others.

We are to be good stewards of the manifold grace of

God. The grace of God here refers to the undeserved favor which He offers to man. The word *manifold* means *many colored*. Phillips speaks of it as *magnificently varied*.

4:11 Even if a man is gifted to preach or teach, he must be sure that the words he speaks are the very words God would have him say on that particular occasion. This is what is meant by "the utterances of God." It is not enough for a man simply to preach from the Bible. He should also have the assurance that he is presenting the particular message intended by God for that audience at that time.

Any man who performs any kind of service should do it with the humble recognition that it is God who empowers him. Then the glory will go to God—to whom it belongs.

A man should not become proud no matter how highly gifted he is in Christian service. The gift was not developed by his own effort, but was given to him from above. In fact, he has nothing which he did not receive. All service should be performed so that God gets the credit.

As Peter points out in v. 11, this honor is presented to God through Jesus Christ as Mediator, and also because of what God has done for us through the Lord Jesus. To this blessed Savior belongs praise and power forever.

XIII/Exhortations And Explanations Concerning Suffering (4:12-19).

A/ An Attitude To Avoid (v. 12): *Beloved, do not be surprised at the fiery ordeal among you, which comes upon you for your testing, as though some strange thing were happening to you;*

B/ A Joy To Experience (v. 13a): *but to the degree that you share the sufferings of Christ, keep on rejoicing;*

C/ A Prospect To Anticipate (v. 13b): *so that also at the revelation of His glory, you may rejoice with exultation.*

D/ A Blessing To Share (v. 14): *If you are reviled for the* name of Christ, you are blessed, because the Spirit of glory and of God rests upon you.

E/ **A Shame To Shun (v. 15):** *By no means let any of you suffer as a murderer, or thief, or evil-doer, or a troublesome meddler;*

F/ **A Privilege To Enjoy (v. 16a):** *but if anyone suffers as a Christian, let him not feel ashamed,*

G/ **An Opportunity To Use (v. 16b):** *but in that name let him glorify God.*

H/ **A Judgment To Expect (v. 17a):** *For it is time for judgment to begin with the household of God;*

I/ **A Contrast To Ponder (v. 17b-18):** *and if it begins with us first, what will be the outcome for those who do not obey the gospel of God? And if it is with difficulty that the righteous is saved, what will become of the godless man and the sinner?*

J/ **A Policy To Follow (v. 19a, RSV):** *Therefore let those who suffer according to God's will do right*

K/ **A Creator To Trust (v. 19b, RSV):** *and entrust their souls to a faithful Creator.*

4:12 The remainder of the chapter contains exhortations and explanations concerning suffering that is incurred for the name of Christ. The word "suffering" and its derivatives are used twenty-one times in this epistle.

The natural attitude for a Christian is to look on persecution as unusual and abnormal. We are surprised when we have to suffer. But Peter tells us that we should look upon it as normal Christian experience. We have no right to expect better treatment from the world than our Savior received. All who desire to live a godly life in Christ Jesus will be persecuted (2 Tim. 3:12).

It is especially true that those who take a forthright stand for Christ become the object of savage attack. Satan doesn't waste his ammunition on nominal Christians. He turns his big guns on those who are storming the gates of Hades.

4:13 The privilege of sharing Christ's sufferings should cause us great rejoicing. We cannot, of course, share His atoning sufferings; He is the only Sin-Bearer. But we can share the same kind of sufferings He endured as a Man. We can share His rejection and His reproach. We can receive the wounds and scars in our bodies which unbelievers would still like to inflict on Him.

If the child of God can rejoice today in the midst of suffering, how much more will he rejoice and be glad when Christ's glory is revealed. When the Savior comes back to earth as the Lion of the tribe of Judah, He will be revealed as the Almighty Son of God. Those who suffer now for His sake will be honored then with Him.

4:14 The early Christians rejoiced that they were counted worthy to suffer shame for His name (Acts 5:41). So should every Christian who has the privilege of being reviled for Christ's sake. Such suffering is a true indication that the Spirit of Glory and of God rests upon us. This is the Holy Spirit who rests upon persecuted Christians as the glory cloud rested upon the tabernacle in the Old Testament, indicating the presence of God.

We know that the Holy Spirit indwells every true child of God, but He rests in a special way upon those who are completely committed to the cause of Christ. They know the presence and power of the Spirit of God as others do not.

4:15 Again Peter reminds his readers that a Christian should never bring suffering upon himself for wrongdoing. He should never be guilty of murder, stealing, evil in general, or meddling in other people's affairs. There is no glory for God in this—only shame for the testimony of Christ.

4:16 But there is no shame connected with suffering for Christ, whether it means "the loss of business, reputation and home; desertion by parents, children and friends; misrepresentation, hatred and even death" (F. B. Meyer). Under the name of *Christian* it is possible to glorify God in all these trials.

4:17 Now Peter contrasts the sufferings of God's people in this life with the sufferings of the wicked in eternity. The time has come for judgment to begin with the household of God. The time referred to is the dispensation of the church, which began at Pentecost and will continue to the rapture. The household of God refers to the church. During this age, the church is undergoing judgment by the unbelieving world. Believers are experiencing their sufferings now, just as Jesus did when He was on earth.

If that is so, what will be the fate of those who do not obey the gospel of God? If Christians suffer now for welldoing, what will the unsaved suffer in eternity for all their ungodly deeds?

4:18 The same argument is contained in this verse, quoted from the Septuagint version of Prov. 11:31: *"And if it is with difficulty that the righteous is saved, what will become of the godless man and the sinner?"*

The righteous man is saved with difficulty. From the divine standpoint his salvation was purchased at enormous cost. From the human standpoint, men are told to "strive to enter by the narrow door" (Luke 13:24). Believers are taught that "through many tribulations we must enter the kingdom of God" (Acts 14:22). With all the dangers and temptations that beset a Christian, it is only a miracle of divine grace that preserves him for the heavenly kingdom.

That being so, what will be the doom of those who have died in their sins, unrepentant and unsaved? A vivid illustration of this truth is found in the following anecdote from the writings of F. B. Meyer:

> It was the earnest wish of a holy man that his death might be so triumphant that his unconverted sons might be convinced and attracted by the evident power of the Gospel to sustain and cheer in the dark passage of the valley. Instead of this, to his deep regret, his spirit lay under a cloud; he was oppressed with fear and misgiving; and the enemy was permitted to torment him to the uttermost. But these very facts were the ones which most profoundly impressed his children. "For," said the eldest, "we all know what a good man our father was; and yet see how deep his spiritual sufferings were. What then may we not expect, who have given no thought to the concerns of our souls?"

4:19 Peter insists that suffering must be according to the will of God. Religious zealots may invite suffering by acting impulsively without divine guidance. Those with a martyr complex tempt God which leads to dishonor. But the true pathway of suffering for a Christian leads to eternal glory. In view of that, he should continue to do right, no matter what the cost may be, and entrust his soul to the faithful Creator.

It seems somewhat strange that Peter should introduce the Lord as Creator here rather than as Savior, High Priest or Shepherd. Christ is our Creator in a twofold sense—we are His as part of the original creation and of the new creation. In either case, we are the objects of His love and care. It is only reasonable that we should trust ourselves to the One who made our souls and who saved them.

5

XIV/Exhortations And Salutations (5:1-14)

A/ To The Elders (vv. 1-4): *Therefore, I exhort the elders among you,*

    1/The Apostle's Credentials (v. 1b)
    a/Elder: *as your fellow-elder*
    b/Witness: *and witness of the sufferings of Christ,*
    c/Partaker: *and a partaker also of the glory that is to be revealed,*
    2/The Elders' Charge (vv. 2-3): *shepherd the flock of God among you,*
    a/Selection (v. 2b): *not under compulsion, but voluntarily, according to the will of God;*
    b/Compensation (v. 2c): *and not for sordid gain, but with eagerness;*
    c/Administration (v. 3): *nor yet as lording it over those alloted to your charge, but proving to be examples to the flock.*
    3/The Elders' Crown (v. 4): *And when the Chief Shepherd appears, you will receive the unfading crown of glory.*

B) To The Younger Ones (v. 5a): *You younger men, likewise, be subject to your elders;*

C/ To All (vv. 5b-11):

1/A Great Virtue (vv. 5b-6): *and all of you, clothe yourselves with humility toward one another, for* God is opposed to the proud, but gives grace to the humble. *Humble yourselves, therefore, under the mighty hand of God, that He may exalt you at the proper time,*

2/A Strong Confidence (v. 7): *casting all your anxiety upon Him, because He cares for you.*

3/A Powerful Enemy (vv. 8-9): *Be of sober* spirit, *be on the alert. Your adversary, the devil, prowls about like a roaring lion, seeking someone to devour. But resist him, firm in your faith, knowing that the same experiences of suffering are being accomplished by your brethren who are in the world.*

4/A Wonderful Promise (v. 10, RSV): *And after you have suffered a little while, the God of all grace, who has called you to his eternal glory in Christ, will himself restore, establish, and strengthen you.*

5/A Worthy King (v. 11): *To Him be dominion forever and ever. Amen.*

D/ Concluding Remarks (vv. 12-14):

1/Scribe (v. 12a): *Through Silvanus, our faithful brother (for so I regard* him), *I have written to you briefly,*

2/Purpose (v. 12b): *exhorting and testifying that this is the true grace of God. Stand firm in it!*

3/Greetings (vv. 13-14): *She who is in Babylon, chosen together with you, sends you greetings, and* so does *my son, Mark. Greet one another with a kiss of love. Peace be to you all who are in Christ.*

5:1 This final chapter of the letter contains exhortations and greetings. First there is a word for the elders. By way of authority for delivering such a charge, Peter introduces himself as a fellow-elder, a witness of Christ's sufferings and a partaker of the impending glory. Fellow-elder—that is a far cry from claiming to be head of the church, isn't it? A witness—Peter saw the Shepherd die for the sheep, and the memory of such love constrains him to care for them as a faithful undershepherd. A partaker—soon the glory will dawn, Christ will appear, and we shall appear with Him in glory (Col. 3:4). Till then the Savior's commission remains, "Tend my lambs! Shepherd my sheep!" (John 21:15-17).

5:2 There is a question among commentators whether verses 2-4 refer to those who exercise spiritual oversight in the local church or to older Christians in general. We feel that the context points strongly to the former as the correct meaning.

Elders are mature men of Christian character who are qualified by the Holy Spirit to provide spiritual leadership in the assembly. The New Testament presupposes a plurality of elders—not one elder over a church or over a group of churches but several elders in one assembly (Phil. 1:1). The qualifications of elders are found in 1 Tim. 3:1-7 and in Titus 1:6-9. In the early church before the New Testament was available in written form, elders were appointed by the apostles and their representatives, but only after sufficient time had elapsed in a new church for it to be evident who had the qualifications. Today Christians should recognize and obey those who have the qualifications and who do the work of elders.

"... Shepherd the flock of God among you." The flock belongs to God but elders have been given the responsibility to serve as undershepherds.

"... Not under compulsion, but voluntarily." Overseeing the flock is not a work into which men are coerced by election or appointment. The Holy Spirit provides the burden and ability, and the elders must respond with a willing heart. So we read in 1 Tim. 3:1, "... if any one aspires to exercise oversight, he desires a good work" (JND). Coupled with divine enablement, must be human willingness.

"... Not for sordid gain, but with eagerness." Financial reward must not be the motive for being an elder. This does not mean that an elder may never be supported by the local church; the existence of such "full-time elders" is suggested in 1 Tim. 5:17-18. But it means that a mercenary spirit is incompatible with true Christian ministry.

5:3 The third phase of Peter's exhortation is this: "nor yet as lording it over those allotted to your charge, but proving to be examples to the flock." The elder should be an example, not a dictator. He should be walking out in front of the flock, not driving them from behind. This strikes at the very heart of authoritarianism.

Many of the abuses in Christendom would be eliminated by simple obedience to the three instructions in vv. 2-3. The first would abolish all reluctance. The second would spell the end of commercialism. The third would be the death of officialism in the church.

5:4 An elder's work involves a tremendous expenditure of physical and emotional energy. He must sympathize, counsel, reprove, rebuke, teach, discipline, and warn. At times it may seem a thankless task. But a special reward is promised to the faithful elder. When the Chief Shepherd appears, he will receive an unfading crown of glory. Frankly, we don't know too much about the promised crowns of Scripture—the crown of exultation (1 Thess. 2:19), the crown of righteousness (2 Tim. 4:8), the crown of life (James 1:12; Rev. 2:10); and the crown of glory. We do not know whether they will be literal crowns that we can cast at the Savior's feet; whether they simply indicate the extent of responsibility that will be given to us during the reign of Christ (Luke 19:17-19); or whether they are facets of Christian character which we will bear throughout eternity. But we do know that they will be ample recompense for any tears, trials and sufferings we have experienced down here.

5:5 Those who are younger, whether in years or in the faith, should be subject to the elders. Why? Because these overseers have wisdom that comes from years of experience in the things of God. They have a deep, experimental knowledge of the Word of God. And they are the ones to whom God has given responsibility for the care of His sheep.

All believers should clothe themselves with humility; it is a great virtue. Moffatt says, "Put on the apron of humility." Very appropriate—since the apron is the badge of a servant. A missionary to India once said, "If I were to pick out two phrases necessary for spiritual growth, I would pick out these: 'I don't know' and 'I am sorry.' And both phrases are evidences of deep humility." Imagine a local church where all the members have this humble spirit; where they esteem others better than themselves; where they outdo each other in performing the menial tasks. Such a church need not be imaginary; it could and should be an actuality.

If there were no other reason for being humble, this would be enough: "God is opposed to the proud, but gives grace to the humble." Here Peter quotes from the Greek version of Proverbs 3:34. Think of it! The mighty God opposed to our pride and determined to break it contrasted with the mighty God powerless to resist a broken and contrite heart.

5:6 This humility is to be shown not only in relation to others but to God as well. In Peter's day the saints were passing through the fires of affliction. These trials, though not sent by God, were permitted by Him. The best policy, Peter says, is to take them humbly from the Lord's hand. He will sustain His people and exalt them in due time.

5:7 The believer is privileged to cast all his anxieties on the

Lord with the strong confidence that He cares. Once again Peter is quoting from the Greek version of the Old Testament—this time from Psalm 55:22.

Worry is unnecessary; there is no need for us to bear the burdens when He is willing and able to bear them for us. Worry is futile; it hasn't solved a problem yet. Worry is sin. A preacher once said "Worry is sin because it denies the love of God; it says that He doesn't care. It denies the wisdom of God; it says that He doesn't know what He's doing. And it denies the power of God; it says that He isn't able to deliver me from whatever is causing me to worry." Something to think about!

5:8 Although we should not worry, we must be sober and watchful, because we have a powerful adversary, the devil. To be sober means to be serious-minded, to take a realistic approach to life, to be intelligent concerning the stratagems of Satan. "An individual who takes no cognizance of the nature or character of the world, one who is unmindful of the purposes and attacks of our adversary, the devil, can afford to live in a lighthearted or flippant way. But for one who sees life as Jesus Christ sees it, there must be an entirely new attitude, an entirely new outlook characterized by sobriety" (Pentecost).

There must also be constant vigilance, a preparedness to meet every attack of the wicked one. Here the adversary is described as a roaring lion, seeking someone to devour. The devil has different poses. Sometimes he comes like a snake, seeking to lure people into moral corruption. Sometimes he disguises himself as an angel of light, attempting to deceive people in the spiritual realm. Here, as a roaring lion, he is bent on terrorizing God's people through persecution.

5:9 We are not to surrender to his fury. Rather we must resist him through prayer and the Word of God. We do not have strength in ourselves to oppose him, but as we are firm in our faith, in our dependence on the Lord, we can resist him.

One of Satan's devices is to discourage us with the thought that our sufferings are unique. As we pass through the fire of affliction, it is easy to faint under the mistaken idea that no one else has as much trouble as we do. Peter reminds us that the same experience of suffering is required of our Christian brothers everywhere.

5:10 True victory in persecution is to see God behind the scenes working out His wonderful purposes. No matter what our trials, we should remember first of all that He is the God of all grace. This lovely title of our God reminds us that His dealings with us are not based on what we deserve, but on His thoughts of love to us. No matter how fierce our testing, we can always be thankful we are not in hell; that is where we ought to be.

A second strong consolation is that He has called us to His eternal glory. This enables us to look beyond the sufferings of this life to the time when we shall be with the Savior and be like Him forever. Just think of it! We have been picked up from the scrap heap and called to His eternal glory!

A third comfort is that suffering is just for "a little while." When contrasted with the eternal glory, life's afflictions are less than momentary.

The final encouragement is that God uses suffering to educate us and mold our Christian character. He is training us for reigning. Three aspects of this training process are listed (see this verse in RSV). They are in the future tense, showing that they are promises, not prayers. God will do it:

> "Restore"—Trials make the believer fit. They supply needed elements in his character to make him spiritually mature.

"Establish"—Suffering makes Christians more stable, able to maintain a good confession, and to bear up under pressure. This is the same word the Lord Jesus used with Peter, "... strengthen (or establish) your brothers" (Luke 22:32).

"Strengthen"—Persecution is intended by Satan to weaken and wear out believers, but it has the opposite effect. It strengthens them to endure.

"The inevitable suffering of the Christian life always yields the same blessed result in the character of believers; it will refine the faith, adjust the character, establish, strengthen and settle the people of God" (Lacey).

5:11 In view of the marvelous way in which God overrules persecution and suffering for His glory and for our good, it is little wonder that Peter bursts into this doxology: "To Him *be* dominion forever and ever. Amen." Only to such a One is glory due, and only in the hands of such a One is dominion safe.

5:12 Silvanus, or Silas, was the one to whom Peter dictated this letter, and probably the messenger who delivered it. The words "as I suppose" in the Authorized Version seem to express some doubt as to his faithfulness. The NASB clears away any such inference by translating the verse: "Through Silvanus, our faithful brother (for so I regard *him*). . . ."

Peter's object in this letter was to assure the Jewish believers of the Dispersion that the Christian faith which they held was the true faith—or, as he calls it, the true grace of God. Perhaps in the heat of persecution, they might be tempted to wonder if they had been right to leave Judaism for Christianity. Peter declares that they were right. They had found God's truth and should stand fast in it.

5:13 "She who is in Babylon, chosen together with you,

sends you greetings, and *so does* my son, Mark."

It is impossible to state with certainty who or what is meant by "She who is in Babylon." Some of the main interpretations are:

    1. The brotherhood (2:17; 5:9). In the Greek the word is feminine.

    2. Peter's wife.

    3. Some local lady of prominence.

It is also impossible to know which Babylon is meant. It could be:

    1. The city on the Euphrates.

    2. A Roman military station by that name on the Nile.

    3. Rome. In Revelation, the city of Babylon is generally understood as referring to Rome (17:1-9; 18:10,21).

A third question arises over the mention of Mark. Is this Peter's own son in the flesh, or is he referring to John Mark, the writer of the Gospel? The latter is more probable. If that is so, then we are left to decide whether Mark was Peter's son because the latter had led him to Christ or whether the word *son* merely designates the close spiritual relationship between an elder and a younger Christian. The word Peter uses for *son* is not the same word which Paul uses to describe his spiritual relationship with Timothy and Titus.

5:14 The epistle closes with a charge and a benediction. The charge is, "Greet one another with a kiss of love." The obligation of brotherly love is a standing order for the church, though the manner of expressing it may vary in cultures and times.

The benediction is, "Peace be to you all who are in Christ." It is a tranquil word to use with storm-tossed saints, who are enduring affliction for the name of Christ. Jesus whispers peace to His blood-bought flock as they suffer for

Him in the midst of a turbulent society.
> Peace, perfect peace, death shadowing us and ours?
> Jesus has vanquished death and all its powers.

Bibliography

Barnes, A.	Notes on the New Testament. *Vol. X. Edinburgh: Blackie & Son, Ltd., n.d.*
Bonar, Andrew R.	Last Days of the Martyrs. *Kilmarnock: John Ritchie, Ltd., n.d.*
Erdman, C. R.	The General Epistles. *Philadelphia: The Westminster Press, 1919.*
Grant, F. W.	Numerical Bible, Hebrews to Revelation. *New York: Loizeaux Brothers, 1903.*
Ironside, H. A.	Notes on James and Peter. *New York: Loizeaux Brothers, 1947.*
Jowett, J. H.	The Redeemed Family of God. *London: Hodder & Stoughton, n.d.*
Lacey, Harry	God and the Nations. *Kilmarnock: John Ritchie, Ltd., c1944.*
Lenski, R. C. H.	The Interpretation of the Epistles of St. Peter, St. John & St. Jude. *Columbus: Wartburg Press, 1945.*
Lincoln, Wm.	Lectures on the First and Second Epistles of Peter. *Kilmarnock: John Ritchie Publ., n.d.*
Lyall, L. T.	Red Sky at Night. *London: Hodder & Stoughton, 1969.*
Meyer, F. B.	Tried by Fire. *London: Morgan & Scott, 1841.*
Pentecost, J. D.	Your Adversary, the Devil. *Grand Rapids: Zondervan, 1969.*
Pollock, A. J.	Why I Believe the Bible is the Word of God. *London: Central Bible Truth Depot, n.d.*
Stibbs, Alan M.	The First Epistle General of Peter. *Grand Rapids: Wm. B. Eerdmans Publishing Co., 1959.*
Westwood, Tom	The Epistles of Peter. *Glendale, Calif.: The Bible Training Hour, Inc., 1953.*
Wolston, W. T. P.	Simon Peter: His Life and Letters. *London: James Nisbet & Co., 1913.*
Young, D. T.	The Unveiled Evangel. *London: Hodder & Stoughton, n.d.*

Bible Versions and Paraphrases

The Authorized Version (King James)
The Revised Version
J. N. Darby's New Translation
F. W. Grant's Numerical Bible
The New American Standard Bible
The New Testament in Modern English by J. B. Phillips
The Holy Bible, edited by Ronald Knox